COCONUT FISTICUFFS

Memoir #2: the 90s

To Buddy,
You'll love it!

J C Scale

by

J.C. Scales

ISBN-13: 978-0-578-68428-4

Contents

This book is for all the curbside heroes, and for the girls who gave us cover as we stole kegs of Meister-Brau from Sigma Beta Tau. For the ones who are too humble to be praised on this paper pedestal and the racist skinheads who don't want to be exposed. Exposed for what they publicly were then and privately are now. Hey skinhead boys, how's that job at the police department goin'? For the college girls who would rather not have the world know about the cotton-mouthed walk of shame out of Teepee Boy's teepee house. I won't name you or even accurately describe you because you don't even exist, do you Becky W?

For all the fatherless violence instigators, tweaked out chronic masturbators, perplexed jailhouse shrinks, and the junkies who think it's all jinxed. All you date rape jocks, and you shit beer-swilling jerkoffs who wear Abercrombie knock-offs. It's for all you Don Rickle pickle punks who recognize yourselves in this book, and you figure you got a piece of the pie coming to you? I'm sorry, does The Goat Lady's Son even know you? All you motherfuckers tried to siphon a part of my soul, and some of you succeeded, but not enough to stop me! Not enough to strangle my optimism! Not enough to make this a book of curses!

I'm sorry for the people I knew who never got up again because they felt too alone and small. I wish I would have stretched out a hand every time and not ever missed an opportunity to shout out some encouragement to you, to cause a distraction…to help you beat back the vampires. Sometimes you get caught up in your own bullshit, man. This is for the lost ones who were cast in the streets completely unprepared, to be devoured like a 2 am burrito, hastily eaten by people who used to be just like them, but who got lucky long enough to get mean.

You go through phases where you blind yourself to the suffering around you to keep from losing your mind. Then, your sense of compassion makes you throw off the blinders and try to save some kid without the wits to make it his first night. You have to give 'em a shower and a falafel, right? Send him to the coffee shop with a fake resume? I gotta at least offer that, don't I? I was him a couple of years ago. The next morning, he's gone from the couch, and so are half my CDs, the front door left wide open. At least he just took the crappy ones. I mean, Van Hagar? He was helping me. He's an angel, a thieving, smelly, little angel.

That's how that song plays when you deal with today's freshly dumpstered youth. The giver gets a little wiser to the ways of the world, and the taker feels a little stronger, knowing that, one time, someone tried to help. There is some value in that, but there has to be a better way. I hope this story can help people to better understand these young people out on the street. To help them peel back the curtains a little bit and see that while they may grimace and strike predatorial poses, those posturings aren't meant for you, they're for the real predators—to bluff them. Look at 'em; they *are* still children. Or they could be again.

It's not just in the slums of Rio de Janeiro, Tijuana, and Detroit. Today in San Francisco—a supposedly elite and progressive city—a mother will sigh in relief that her 13yo daughter is finally old enough to pimp out. In ten years, when that poor child is too far into adulthood to sell it for decent sums of money, she will just trade it for small amounts of drugs to take her out of herself until she lucks out and overdoses for keepsies. Maybe it's a 9yo kid in wealthy Pacific Heights cutting herself because her mom was unhappy when she lost a stupid horse jumping competition. It's all of these kids! Even the ones who are inside and we think are safe. They are subconsciously unhappy and insecure about this world's grim future. They go running inside their iPads, iPhones, reality shows, and video games. It's the new way of closing your eyes and covering your ears! *You can't see me!* With this new generation, it's not a five-minute game that a 3yo plays; it's everyone who is 3-30—and at this point, they're planning on doing it forever!

The youth of today know in their souls that when it comes time to inherit the earth, their parents are seriously thinking of handing them a globe-sized empty toothpaste tube. In their minds, they are screaming, *Hey! We're getting screwed out of our world, so a few old pieces of shit can concentrate all the world's wealth; plant* **and** *chemical! Turn it all into a few diamonds of consolidated power? Just so a few Gollums can go hide in a cave with it? My Precious! My Precious!*

Is that what Gollum was? A hedge fund manager? Good call! Some of those old English dudes really nail it. Hey, Pfizer Pharmaceutical Corporation! My niece found out what pills you want to get her hooked on before her Sweet Sixteen party. She said, "Sit and spin! Sit and fuckin' spin!"

Taking into consideration most of what I just said, it is hard to imagine any good happening, but it does. Every day, a little girl gets a pet. She can't sleep all night! She's mentally designing matching paper hats for her and her sheep to wear. Every day, a coke-addled high school dropout catches a third-class bus from Tijuana to Puerto Vallarta and becomes the assistant chef in a Hari-Krishna temple. And does it without becoming a Hari-Krishna—that was me!—then stays for six months and not only doesn't do blow he writes a screenplay, then makes a movie! A semi-crappy one, but hey, it's a start to much better things.

Some of the stories that spill through the streets of the world every day would make Oliver twist his leg straight. This book promises to deliver enough rays of hope to counterbalance the all too often harsh realities of daily life. After all, it is also true that the streets tell stories of love and victory. They are full of hopeful mothers who will never give up.

Some clues will be slightly changed in this book to protect identities of the guilty, shy or stupid. Also, there's a thing called sarcasm that no one seems to understand anymore. I will distill long conversations as accurately as possible without contriving. Don't worry yourself about that stuff during the read; by the end, we will have a highly accurate account of what happened. Don't go all *Oprah* on me if I say, "I think Heroin Dan might have been an alien." I can't wait until you jokers discover who Hunter S. Thompson is. *Prove the bats were there, Hunter!* All of the main dramatic points will be pretty much exact. That part will be simpler due to the intensity of those moments. They changed our lives, our eyes wide open to them. We even wished to forget many of those instants, unable to, as we cold sweat out another nightmare of that evening from a large, indelible fear folder in our brains. But honestly, most of it was a fun party.

Read this, and realize that growing up in the streets all scrappy and unkempt is nothing to be ashamed of, pitied, spited, or feared. We were just kids whose parents got broke or unlucky, likely both, and probably not in that order. The most beautiful and authentic people I have met in this world are what you might call *"poetic guttersnipes from hell, with ripped up flannels and a bit of a smell."* Like our Uncle Steinbeck said, "If you need help in this world go to the poor. They are the only ones that will help you with no strings attached…the only ones." All right, just read the thing.

Paradise Unflossed

I am sitting in my new living room, and it's unbelievable how well my life is going. So good, I don't even suspect it's a trick. It's the early nineties, and I'm legally allowed to drink in bars now. Kurt Cobain is still alive, and the Rodney King Riots just tore LA a new asshole. Bill Clinton just made George Bush Sr. a one-termer, and as a reward to himself, he will soon be getting hummers from an intern. As the cigar dampens, it is rumored she yelled, "Stick it in my Oval Office, Slick Willie!"

No one has cell phones or Wi-Fi yet. It's fucking great! I paid my pound of pride to the dark gods and never joined their side. It's time to collect my karma credits. Life is real good back then. 971 E. Carrillo is the warm tropical island that I weathered all these storms for.

I am with Greg, aka "G-Money," a new roommate, and my pot dealer. I literally only have to walk down the hall to get more weed. He is sitting next to me, and we are about to fire up a video game in the living room. Just outside is a view of the red Spanish tile-roofed city of Santa Barbara, with all its greenery. Just beyond that, the waves of the Pacific beckon us to a lifetime of frolic and fortune.

I am living here with my first girlfriend. She is the most perfect thing ever to happen to an unfortunate gutter kid like me. She is a fucking saint, and I'll punch anyone in their lying mouth who says otherwise. She has loving, light blue eyes, a sleek, Irish jawline, and light blonde hair that stops at the shoulders. Basically, like a hotter, Laura Dern. Long perfect legs, and tits that would make Stevie Wonder wreck his car. What is Stevie Wonder doing driving a car, you ask? The bus wasn't fast enough to have someone describe my woman's bikinied love melons at Ledbetter Beach to him. She is prettier than shit and supremely confident in who she is. She hasn't had it easy herself, practically raising her younger sister as a forced favor to her *carefree* mother. I love her so fucking much! At the moment, she is waitressing at The Paradise Café, delivering steaming bowls of rock shrimp fettuccini in a timely fashion, and breaking all the hearts in her tight white shorts.

Presently, on the home front, it's just me, Greg, and this smoky bong. After I hand Greg this ass whooping on Sega Golf, we are going down to La Super Rica on Milpas. Thanks to my newfound money flow, I can afford to get a few tacos with my burrito. After smoking five or six hits out of this two-footer, I will probably need a series of tacos covering each farmyard category.

Greg looks at the bong, "JC, you left a goddamn ghost in the machine again." This means I left smoke in the bong; I didn't clear it, a party foul, but screw it, I just made $200 in one transaction and didn't have to leave the house to do it. Good old Walter, who always buys a bunch of weed every other day, came over and paid the highball price, as it was my last pound. I don't really sell pounds because it puts you on a fancier cop radar, as if ounces aren't bad enough. They're both felonies, but one gets you tossed in county jail, and the other one can get you a prison term. An ounce level dealer is more likely to rat you out if he gets caught.

You see, an ounce is that magic quantity where you get in massive trouble—three to six months in county jail—in the early nineties. Imagine going to jail for that long for a single sandwich bag full of pot. If your daddy can pay for a halfway decent lawyer? Don't sweat it, but I'm not ballin' lawyer money, that's for sure. Right now, my dad wouldn't buy me a hand towel to wipe piss off my face.

I respond to Greg's previous accusation of leaving too much smoke in the bong. "You couldn't make that hit that you're about to take any less nasty if you let Tipper Gore censor it. Did you buy it straight from the donkey's asshole or what?" This is a reference to the fact that he bought it in Tijuana. Greg is in the habit of buying five or ten pounds of the dirty dirt weed on the other side, casually walking across the border into San Diego, then taking the Amtrak train back up to Santa Barbara. In the summers, you can get ten times your original investment that way. Not bad, huh?

Greg is savvy. You wouldn't know from listening to or looking at him, though. A big toucan nose, long brown roots leading to platinum bleached hair that shoots out in unlikely directions. He always wears baggy denim cargo shorts that he washes quite a bit actually because he's continuously getting little bits of puke on them. Oh yeah, Greg is a puker *and* a chew-spitter. When we moved in together, I didn't know I would find him in the living room four times a week with empty Bud tallboys piled up around his ankles. Often with chew spit slowly dripping onto his Santa Cruz t-shirt, creating a pool of soggy, smelly brown toxicity that acts as a growing clock for how long he's been like that. If the chew spit drool has only made a pancake sized circle on his shirt, it's only been an hour or so, you can leave him like that for a bit. If you have a drool circle, the size of a Rusty's Pizza? Better wake him up before it starts infecting the couch.

Fuckin' great guy, though. We call him G-Money because he knows how to grow money from nasty brown, seedy bricks. He allows me to do it as well because the wholesale prices he extends to me are precisely why I'm doing so well in life lately. I would cut someone for trying to roll him. Hell, sometimes I even tell him he's pretty.

In the early nineties, pot grown in the outdoors is pretty much only harvested once a year around Halloween, and that gets smoked up by Christmas break. As far as indoor weed, no one has the start-up money for all the equipment. In the primitive early days of indoor pot-growing, you were likely to burn down your house, then go to prison for five years for attempted cultivation. This is because the courts have a significant hard-on for pot around here. Authority types—of which we have more than our fair share per capita—are convinced it makes upper-class daughters horny for long-haired boys with unwashed nut sacks and empty bank accounts. If you drive a VW Van in Santa Barbara in 1993 and you look like you know where the party is? Expect to get pulled over by some crew-cutted slap-jack with a penchant for cruelty and a habit for failing with the ladies. It is a dangerous game, Greg and I are playing, but we feel invincible. Things have been going swimmingly, so why should we doubt it? I'm four strokes ahead as we start the back nine. "Greg?"

"What?"

"I'm driving this ball so far down the fairway it's going to bounce out the back of the TV and roll down the hill to 7-11. Then, I am going to do a little dance on this coffee table, making cock gestures towards your stupid mouth." I'm not really going to do that because I'm way slouched back into the couch, and I plan on staying that way until this game is over.

Greg isn't really fazed because he doesn't give a shit about much, much less video golf. And to be honest, it's showing in how he plays. G-Money mulls over the insult, perhaps devising a plan to trip me off the table or punch me in the nuts should I try to attempt anything overly celebratory. "I would smoke you on a real course," he retorts with his trademark snort. "This is nothing like real golf. In fact, knowing how to play real golf is a disadvantage at this weak attempt to recreate the feeling of a 300-yard drive in the open air. I smell literally no fresh-cut grass right now." Greg is getting worked up, just like I predicted. He's just getting started, "Where are the golf carts? There are certain requirements to call something golf! It's preposterous to call this that, that's all I'm saying. Utterly absurd."

I ease up a bit because we still have a lot of game left, and I don't want him to quit. "Seven more holes, and I'll buy you a super carnitas burrito, G-Money. Until then, can you try to take this seriously and stop sucking so much? I'm trying to break some course records here. When you suck so bad, it kind of starts bleeding into my game. *Capiche?*"

"Well, stop yappin' and get to tappin'. This one's going in the lake," says Greg wrongly.

"Yeah, sure it is," I spout annoyingly. "I'm going to destroy your nut sack on this fucking drive, G-Money. Then, my short game is going to make it start popping, like Jiffy-Pop kernels."

Now, I've cracked Greg's veneer. His response is stilted, stuttered and stalled, much like his attempts to get out of sand traps. "What the fuck? Salvador Dali pissed into your brain or what? What the fuck's that even mean?"

"It means you should probably butter up your nut sack because it's JIFFY-POP TIME!" In some ways, my maturity has been stunted by PTSD during crucial development years. This should be clear to you by now.

Toc! I almost drive the green from the tee on a four par.

Knock! Knock! Knock! It's the front door. The visitors don't wait for a response, and the door swings forcefully open. Through the haze of pot smoke, I can see the multiple glints of gunmetal. It's the cops.

Jail

Fuckin' Walter, man. How did I not see it? Of course, Walter was ratting me out. Why was he so desperate to overpay for a pound? The fuckin' prick had cops down the block, that's why. He has always been weird. How the fuck am I supposed to know why he's acting strange this time? You're blind to the flaws of people who have stacks of money they are trying to give you anyway. Why am I such an idiot? My life was amazing for only two years? After all that! Fuck. Age 4-12 wasn't terrible, I guess. But collectively, that's only ten years out of 20? That were good?! When I say it like that, it doesn't seem so bad; an even break. But, look at the low points, they are so low and seem so well-timed to slow any momentum, to crush any dreams before they can ever get past the caterpillar stage. I just can't take any more losses. My hands start to tremble from stress, as if they were only on hold, mid-shake, from the old days. Shaky Scales was one of my many nicknames back then. Hungover, hungry, and stressed. Now, the shakes are back after a brief two-year hiatus, and they're going to stay for a while. I feel like crying, but I can't. There are people here. I let my soul climb into a lonely hole and cry itself raw.

Getting booked into the county clink only takes a few hours, and I'm placed in a non-gang member tank. Mostly 2nd DUI's, bar fighting, stealing, bad checks, and pissing dirty at the probation office. Despite these lightweight rap sheets, everybody still acts all macho because no one wants to be punked like a bitch.

It's hard not to look a little nervous as you sit and wait for the gate to open and let you into the day room area where your new roommates sit at a half-dozen aluminum picnic tables. People play cards, dominoes, write letters, read, formulate lies to tell their public defender, or stare into space.

At the closest table to where I can view my new home through the jail bars, is an artist decorating the back of other inmate's envelopes using water-dipped M&M's like a watercolor brush to fill in the penciled outlines of impeccable Cholo art. Running the wet candy inside the flowing lines, he gets a pretty good amount of coloring into the envelope mural. Once that's finished, he pops the pale M&M into his mouth and picks through the bag for the next color he needs. *Not enough browns in here, ese.* For the cost of three Snickers, this probation violating Picasso will paint you putting the pedal to the metal on a top-down '64 *Impala* while your faithful woman points a sawed-off shotgun out the back at the pursuing cops. Your woman gets that in the mail with *your* love letter inside? She would be a fool not to wait for you. And for only three Snickers? *Sheeeit!* Andy Warhol used to charge more than that to spit in your drink.

I finally hear the mechanical buzz that shortly precedes the barred gate sliding sideways. I step forward into the room as all these assholes stare at me, wondering what I would do if they took all my Top Ramens. I puff up my chest a bit, which backfires when I'm clearly not sure where I should go at first with my cardboard box full of basic hygiene shit, clothes, sheets, and an impossibly thin blanket. A white dude, who has been waiting for me to get to him in my quick scan of potentially friendly faces, motions me over.

Three bunk rooms adjoin to the day room. Each has its own sliding steel bar gates which lock 12 to 16 men inside after 8 pm each night, leaving the day room empty. One bunk room for each color of the County Jail rainbow: Brown, black, and the one I'm going to. The rules of jail are numerous but straightforward. Stay with your color, keep your head down, and when you take a shit in front of everybody, you better time the flush just as the turd hits the water. Being in a non-gang member tank, these rules are slightly more relaxed, except for the flush timing. It's weird taking a shit while two guys are less than a yard from you, talking about if we're going to be allowed to watch the Superbowl or not. You get used to it, like most things you thought you never would.

The second day I'm in there, we get this skinhead-lite looking guy in our bunk room, and he immediately goes about organizing assignments for people to bring back certain foods from the cafeteria. He has the rotation of the menu memorized from the last ten times he's been in here. Next thing you know, he's gotten his hands on a shit ton of sugar packets, wheat bread slices, and fruit. This all goes into a bucket he somehow procured to ferment into Pruno—jailhouse liquor, you know, toilet gin.

People are starting to love this guy. We are bonded in pulling the wool over the jail guard's eyes, and we're going to get drunk at the end. The next day, he has us bring back bananas and spinach, which he proceeds to start drying to be smoked in a toilet paper roll pipe. He's pretty convincing that soon we are all going to be higher than a shaman at his own birthday party. He gives us a preview of what to expect.

"You gotta hold in the smoke for a long time. The banana gives you a psychotropic high." He super enunciates and draws out, "Psycho-t-r-a-a-w-p-i-c-c," before continuing the bullshit fest to his group of rapt, new disciples. "And the spinach has a light weed high. Both of them together are strong enough to get you ripped." He's got them on the hook. "Then, we'll have the Pruno by the weekend. It's gonna be a party, guys. Fuck this place, we're *flyyyin'* into space."

This guy loves being loved. He has developed the gift of gab, which he uses mostly as a delivery service for hollow promises to get people liking him and on board with his flop agendas. This affection, along with the goal of a common cause with his newfound friends, fills the hole in his heart where some daddy hugs should have probably gone. Guys like him are manipulatable and usually entertaining. I determine him to be a net gain for our bunk room.

Just pretend to like guys like this twice as much as you really do, and their tongue starts wagging. I am wondering how he will eventually get himself rolled up out of here to an isolation tank, i.e., temporary solitary confinement. He is fat and sloppy, with a flattened red nose that looks tiny on his giant potato head. His eyes are permanently crossed from what my spider tinglings are telling me was a heroin overdose. He has muscular arms from the hard labor job he is about to lose for not showing up at, yet again. His gingivitis is terrifying, and he is incapable of picking up on simple social cues, such as when you wince away from his corn toothed mouth when it tries to start a black market business with you.

As far as bunkmates in jail? This is as good as it gets. When living in a 250 sq. foot room with 12 or more dudes, you have to be tolerant, unless you want to fight all the time. And due to the tight proximity, it's hard not to notice the shortcomings that led these societal castaways to such a house of failed opportunity.

Some of the other guys can't wait for the booze to be ready or even just for the banana peels and spinach to dry. They are activated now and have once again become slaves to their thirsty dopamine receptors. In their frenzy, they chop up some lines of Comet cleanser and start snorting it for the intense burn, which gives them a sort of horrendous, methy, placebo high. I'm incredulous. They offer me some, "Come on, man. Are you a nerd or something?"

This is one of the easier forms of peer pressure I've resisted. "Aw, no guys. I tore out my septum on a big pile of Peruvian a while back. I've got to rest up for a while."

However, they are characteristically persistent little tweakers. They want me to sink to their level of depravity so no one can look down on anyone else. Their little raggedy sub-crew is still outnumbered in our bunk room by the guys, not currently snorting cleanser. Faith in humanity restored. It's not like they can really push the issue that hard. Or can they? "You want to shoot it?"

Fuck.

A week later, it turns out a new guy has smuggled in some meth in his *rent by the minute hole.* The meth rats almost rip and tear it directly from the inside of his butt. When a guy who has meth inside of his anus is waving you guys back like *you* are the rabid zombie, and he is saying, "Calm down, you fucking junkies!" I have news for you, and it's super terrible.

A few hours later, the shower cleaner is gone, and the banana peels and spinach are deemed dry enough to smoke. The flabby buff B-team skinner prepares us for takeoff. It's myself, the meth rats, Ricky the former high school football star turned coke head, and Daryl Banks, the black dude that we have adopted because he had a problem with a much larger dude in the black tank. He's funny, a nerd from Chicago that's in here for selling crack, even though he doesn't do drugs or drink. He and Ricky are friends from the outside, so he's here with us now.

Skinner Boy has scrounged up a piece of tin foil and has turned it into a crude pipe along with the previously mentioned toilet paper roll. Now, he has a bowl of fresh spinach. We couldn't procure matches, so he's carved the wood off of a pencil, leaving only the lead that was inside, and broken that into one-inch sections. One of these is twisted at the end of a strip of toilet paper to be dropped into the center of a slightly removed TV plug's prongs. When the graphite lead touches both of these prongs at the same instant, you get a *poof!* The lead explodes in a chemical reaction and lights the toilet paper afire. Skinner boy does this, and it promptly shorts out the electricity in our entire tank. TV, ceiling lights, everything. Suddenly, it's close to pitch black. We only see the flaming toilet paper light up the flab skinner's face as he greedily sucks down the only hit anyone will be taking that day.

The next day, he is dragged out after an unknown culprit rats him out. He's led out of our tank by two guards to the tune of me singing, *"He's good to the finish, 'cause HEEE smokes his spinach…he's Popeye the Sailllor Man! Toot-toot!"*

It gets a decent laugh. Popeye turns and smiles, feeling loved enough to have been nicknamed. I never see Popeye again after that. I imagine he is in the Peruvian jungle, looking for different things to smoke and take detailed notes on. I wish him well. Remember to pack the lizards into the pipe tail first, Popeye.

A Letter from My Baby!

It's true! That line above! In general, I am one of the more hyper-divulgent people you'll ever come across, but out of respect for Shawna, I think I'll keep the contents of that letter private. Let's just say it's sweet, furious at the cops, and sexy in all the right places. It's the thing I needed most in the world right now. The last two mail calls got me pretty sad when my name wasn't called. I didn't count on the guards taking their sweet time checking the letters for blotter acid. I am sure they all crowd around the guard who knows how to read, and they get a good laugh out of our wives', mothers' and girlfriends' collective, dedicated anguish. "Ha, look at this one. Darla writes, 'Oh Randy, it's so hard to sleep without you. I bunch up the pillows on your side of the bed, and when I wake up and realize it's not you, I cry and shake. I will be strong Randy, but nothing feels like you.'"

"Ha! I got news for you, Darla. Randy is goin' to the joint! You better build a better Randy scarecrow, ya dumb bitch."

"*Hardy hardy hoo-haw!* Good one, Sarg! *Hardy-snort-squeal-hardy-suey-snort!*"

The guards' break room at jail must have the lamest and cruelest banter since the Vatican cafeteria on Spaghetti Thursday.

After finishing my letter, I am bolstered with hope and that fantastic feeling of walking on air like when me and Shawna used to walk holding hands. She's going to wait for me! Even if the prosecutor gets their two years in prison.

Wait! There's a picture! A cute, tasteful, yet sexy wallet-sized of her sitting on a park bench, smiling and offering me hope. I hide it under the letter before anyone can see. I heard a story about a guy that went to court, and when he got back, some piece of shit had rifled through his belongings, found a picture of his girl, jacked off onto her face, then stuck it face down on the wall above his pillow. Clearly, the guy went berserk when he got back. He identified his chief suspect, and I heard they went at it in the day room with the PVC shower curtain poles like felonious Jedis.

This would **never** happen to *my* precious Shawna's face. Hell no! I put her photo and sweet letter in a Ziploc and carry it everywhere, slyly tucked into my waistband. You would have to kill me for this picture. If these animals knew the rowdy hotness level of my lady, they just might try.

I do have one letter I can read to you, though. It's from my 15yo little sister, Hannah. It has a tiny sticker of a rodent wearing a bowtie in the upper-righthand corner—a secret code, I'm certain. I'm sure she sang it out in her head as she wrote it. I never know it at the time, but singing things out might be a symptom of her multiple learning disabilities. Why can't all symptoms be beautiful like this? Her letter goes, *"J.C., I hooope you enjoy being 22. I'm sure you'll love my weird bag I made you with looooots of love. It took me over a month. I'll bring it to you sooooon. It has secret compaaaaartments!"*—in case the code wasn't clear enough.

"Hey, J.C.? Mom's Mr. Magoo 'cause we don't have any windshield wipers, so when we driiiive in the rain, we're virtually bliiiiind. Oh yeah, Chicky Boy knows how to crow. He started in the trunk one morning when we were sleeping in the caaaaar."

What could be more precious than letters in jail?

"Hey, J.C.? We saw a 20-pound gopher in Ohiiiio, it was scary. Chicken Girl had eggs. They might hatch. I sure hope sooooo. Then I'd have babies running aaaaall around the Cadillaaaaac. Well, take care, we're on our way. Bye, Sweetie."

The Big Court Date

The day arrives when I go to see what kind of bullshit they want from me for selling an herb that helps people relax in a frantic world. The prosecutor is dead set on sending me to prison because of all the resisting arrests and whatnot from my Isla Vista days. In the eyes of the court, these aren't as far behind me as I considered them to be myself. Tales of teenage excess and authoritarian resistance have followed me all the way downtown. Seems unfair. All that shit was like eight miles away and four years ago. Grudge holders.

The judge arrives and gives me the up and down as I stand for judgment. I plead, "Not guilty." Saying I'm guilty would mean I'm admitting I had done something wrong. Guilty of being a thoughtful caretaker of my community, perhaps. I'll plead guilty to that. Do you want to send me to reverse jail? All expenses paid to Brazil for three weeks? Sign me up. Other'n that? Kick rocks, you creepy robed pervert. Never trust a man in a robe unless it's made out of terrycloth and he's holding a White Russian.

My public pretender stutters out an attempt to save me from the precarious possibility of my becoming pink slime for the prison industry. "Your Honor, my client has expressed a desire to help children. We would like to call his girlfriend to the stand."

Thank god I came up with this sham to pull everyone's heartstrings. In the back of the room, where the public is sitting, is my crew of supporters: Shawna, my amazing portrait of a dutiful and faithful girlfriend. Brandon Chapman, in a shiny buttoned-up shirt, no less. Sarah Bauer, showing her protective and unwaveringly stern face for the whole room to see. All of them dressed up and ready to support in any way possible, including a possible dramatic courtroom escape if you judge things by the look my mom, The Goat Lady of Isla Vista, is sporting. "You let my boy go! He didn't do nothin' wrong ta nobody!" she says, as per usual at these events. I hear her voice fade out of the room as she's led out for a moment to talk with the bailiff.

On the stand where my girlfriend, no, my fiancé, now sits, my public pretender tries to remember how to talk, "Shawna Kogenberger? You are J.C.'s fiancé?"

"Yes," Shawna responds convincingly. I want it to really be true, just as soon as I can prove myself worthy of such an ambitious title.

"And you are pregnant with his child?" goes the public pretender again.

Shawna answers quickly, and so confidently, she even tricks me for a second, "Yes."

The court gets quiet for a minute, mulls it…and buys it! Other things are said, but they don't matter compared to that second that she sold the goods to the judge and everyone else. I am about to be released on my own recognizance. This means I am not considered a flight risk, and I don't have to post bail. Once we leave the antique, picturesque Santa Barbara Courthouse—whose visage lies to you about the cruelty of its purpose, much like its sister postcard, the Santa Barbara Mission—it will be less than 24 hours until I'm in her arms.

Shawna and I make love like the first ashes of Vesuvius are falling on us, and there is no time to escape anything but a final, aggressive frolic through the erotic alphabet of our libidos. We Pompeii the night away. That she was willing to do that to get me out only made me love her more. Is that even possible?

It's only a month or so before the case is resolved, and our temporary respite is over. I am to report to the county jail for a 90-day sentence. Not a bad result considering that's down from two years in prison. Thanks, baby!

If I have ever said I don't have white privilege, then remind me of this day in court. If Shawna and I didn't look like the poster couple for caucasity, then I would have ended up in Susanville Prison for sure. Not to discount the level of charm we threw down, but let's be honest, white people who look like splendid examples of Aryan superiority are treated more fairly in American courts; most others are not. I don't wish that light sentence overturned, and in the early 1990s, it's lenient for red-handed sales of marijuana, but I do feel obligated to fight for others to be treated more fairly as well. Of course, I do.

That same day, the 19yo Mexican chained to me gets five years for a non-violent offense like it's nothing. I feel the last of his hope drain and twitch away as the judge says the number, "To be remanded for a period of five years in a state correctional facility." His mother simultaneously begins sobbing in anguish three rows to the left of us as the judge continues on without a second's respect for the solemnity of the moment. It's like he's calling out a fuckin' sandwich order. This boy will come out of prison changed; his youth gone. He will be stoic, withdrawn, disturbed, and potentially violent. His mom knows it, and she's helpless to it. I almost feel worse for the mothers than the boys. You are sentencing her too. And for what? He had some chemicals that make poverty seem less terrible for a few hours? Fuck you, Your Honor.

So, back to the same tank as before. To get my old bunk back, I promise three ramens when the next commissary arrives. I settle in, more comfortable than last time because now I know my destiny at least. 90 days really means 70 days unless they catch you with pills taped to your dick.

I just have to stick to myself and get mentally healthy, so I can figure out a legal way to make money when I get out that doesn't involve licking The Man's boots. Everyone always loved my abstract paintings with Jim Morrison, Bob Marley, and Jimi Hendrix. I order some colored pencils and a drawing tablet off commissary, along with a half dozen each of Top Ramens and Snickers. Everyone likes animals, so I develop a style of drawing them in a tattoo tribal/Pacific Northwest Indian style, with plenty of my own inventive flairs blended in. I am going to make t-shirts and sell them for double what they cost to make. Turns out, I still got it, and that's what I do at the stainless-steel picnic tables all day while dominos slap loudly down all around me: tigers, buffalos, iguanas, monkeys, and raccoons. The whole forest, desert, and backyard.

I'm a pretty funny guy, and while skinny, I have uncanny wire strength and a disaster yielding left hook. I'm pretty confident I can use these resources to make it by in here. By the second week, I already have some nicknames. The Mexicans call me El Tigre because of my back tattoo, which is actually supposed to be a bear, but since I gave the bear thumbs, I'm El Tigre now. The brothers call me Hollywood because I'm handsome, I guess. Good thing I didn't do that prison stretch. My gorgeous pooper would have suffered so much abuse, by week two, it would have looked like a firecracker went off in a chili-cheeseburger.

Don't get me wrong, some of the guys in county jail have been to the joint, and they don't have a mechanism in their brain that adjusts the rules for the different styles of lockups they visit. It's just, *Am I in a cage? If not, do I want to engage in behavior that might prevent me from visiting a cage by late this evening? If the answer is 'yes, I AM in a cage,' well then, IT'S BEAST LYYFFFEE!!!!'*

That's why I get a little scared for this new kid in here with a big ass mouth. We name him Montana because—you guessed it—he's from Montana. He's about 20 and got caught selling fake acid in Skinhead Square down on State Street. This makes me kind of like him. He's an entertaining guy. But he's as naïve as an AIDS patient voting for Reagan. The very same Reagan who lives up on a ranch in the mountains here in Santa Barbara, right down the road from Michael Jackson, the creepy hitmaker who lures children into Neverland with the help of his trusty, secret-keeping monkey, Bubbles.

Ok, back to the subject at hand: the problem with Montana is his mouth is louder than me on the outside, and this is the *inside*. This attracts the attention of Cortez, the low self-esteem wannabe gangbanger with a significant carbohydrate addiction. He weighs about 280, and it's not a well carried 280. Some of us have nicknamed him Vato the Hutt.

Montana and him have a few back and forths that end in nothing until one morning, Cortez comes bursting into our bunk room with a shank and tackles Montana, stabbing him with his sharpened toothbrush handle repeatedly. Montana doesn't realize he's being stuck.

I'm lying on my lower bunk two-feet away from them, and I'm suddenly forced to position myself to not die if they collapse on me, legs ready to kick away what might be a massive job for them. Ricky, Montague and Marlboro are chanting for blood at the edge of it all, laughing, and screaming like assholes. It's a boring life here, so this is a highly welcomed, non-pay-per-view match.

Montana isn't doing much. He might be getting injured from all the stabs. Suddenly, it appears he was just bolstering himself. He releases a rapid flurry of hooks and jabs into the hateful flab mound, causing it to quiver and shake. He connects a half dozen times, and blood spurts out from Cortez's face like jelly from a giant, lumpy donut. Cortez drops the shank as he takes a full blow to the center of his face. He's done.

"MONTANA!!!"

The crowd goes nuts as Montana is standing in the center of the day room, sucking up all the love with a big dumb smile on his face. Meanwhile, Cortez slinks back to his empty bunk room to stick toilet paper up his bloody nose and ruminate on what possibly could have gone wrong.

Who would have thought? I look to Montana's ribs, expecting to see a vast pool of blood from all the stabbings. We lift his shirt, and it just looks like a series of little bitch ass mosquito bites. What the fuck? I pick up the shank. It's been sharpened in a highly bullshit fashion. Rubbed on the cement until its sharpest point was barely more intimidating than a wet Q-tip. It seems like calorie counting isn't the only area where Cortez is lazy.

I've got to hand it to him. I had my Ramens on the chubby kid like everyone else. Now, of course, we're all pretending like that was never true. We continue high fiving and slapping the back of the unlikely boxing champ from Montana like we knew it all along.

Figuring Out A New Way

On one of my last nights, the Mexicans throw boiling water on a guy because he has a giant pentagram tattooed on his back. These Mexicans have Jesus tattoos all over and believe if they ask him for forgiveness from time to time, then they can deal all the coke and speed they want. Also, you must punish the satanic when the opportunity presents itself.

Waking up to agonized screams is disturbing. Hard to get back to sleep. The guards come and take him out, and I feel claustrophobic as fuck. I need out of this place. It's been over two months, and I feel myself going crazy again like in juvie. I just want to be out with my girlfriend, no…my fiancé. I know that being in her arms will make me feel human again.

The day comes, and I get home. Sarah and Brandon are there. Being the primary dealer, Greg got understandably freaked out, and he's left back to Isla Vista, where it's safe. But not before leaving his room to Sarah and Brandon. **Where is she?!** *Where is my love?* I see her appear in the doorway shyly, all dressed up and with lipstick. This is going to be the most fabulous night of my life. Like when you're sick, then you get better, and you go snowboarding, and you feel extra remarkable in comparison to the horrid situation of yesterday. I highly recommend suffering sometimes to give you some contrast. You're only as good as the distance you climbed for your victories.

We bang like wild, ferocious animals. Flesh is ripped, and fluids are sipped. By the time I'm done servicing her immaculate little whisker biscuit, it looks like the remnants of a losing attempt at a biscuits and gravy eating competition. Two months of pent up jail tension has been released upon it in a spontaneous flurry of thrusting, tossing, twisting, jerking, and spurting. I cum about two ounces of saved up gizz, and my dick shows no sign of softening. I plunder on, letting the cum add to the lubrication, as mucousy strands of it run up and down my shaft like white yarn strings dancing on an accordion.

I leave my love's plundered treasure cave to recover and go about choosing the designs I drew in jail. I'm going to produce a series of t-shirts and make a million bucks. I borrow $1,200 from Shawna to cover it, figuring once the first bunch is sold, I can pay her back and create a new round of shirts. This is assuming I don't spend a dime on anything else. I start with the drawing titled, *Descent upon the Oblivious.* It's an eagle about to snatch up a rabbit. Next is *Iguana with Grasshoppers.* Lastly, we have *Indian Brave with Buffalo.* These are all excellent designs. Of course, I should make a living as an artist! Within a few weeks, I watch my designs get laid down one color at a time on a spinning silkscreen daisywheel at Arosha's Silk Screening, in an old WW2 shack, just off of State Street. It is quite intoxicating the first time an artist sees their work being mass-produced right in front of them that way. I'm giddy with anticipation. "Keep those screens handy," I tell them, "I'll be back soon for more!"

I bundle up my shirts of all colors and sizes and go out into the streets to sell them. Business isn't too bad. People like them. Early on, the

Midnight Sun, a head shop on State Street, agrees to carry them. The problem is that I have to use the money I make to simply get around town and eat. Naturally, lugging around a bunch of shirts in the sun requires a few beers from time to time as well. Shirt slinging is thirsty work.

Within two months, I'm out of shirts and short on rent. Shawna tells me it's time to get a real job. I have never done anything but sell pot, so I'm at a loss. I have no resume at all, and I'm scared someone's mom will recognize me if I get a job on State Street. They'll for sure call the manager to warn them about the kid who pissed off their balcony onto the dog on Easter Sunday that one year.

Adding to my problems is that I am on felony probation, and I have to call a number every day, and if the code: Red 1-2-3 comes up on the prerecorded message, then I have five hours to get my piss clean. This is not a super huge problem because I have a secret weapon, Naturally Clean Herbal Tea. You drink a gallon of this stuff before you go in, and you'll be pissing clearer than a Yosemite waterfall. **Do not** buy the mango flavor, though! Your probation officer will be standing right beside you as the bathroom fills up with the smell of mangoes. They may ask you point-blank, "Why does your piss smell like penis colada?" It would be a legitimate inquiry.

Also, there are to be surprise visits to my house. *Yippee!* This wouldn't usually be a problem except that Sarah is growing pot in our backyard. Now, Sarah is a woman who isn't looking to purchase any bullshit. She feels it is her right as an American to grow a harmless herb in her yard. It doesn't seem to bother her that I'm on felony probation for doing something similar. That she was putting us all at unnecessary risk didn't seem to faze her. She kind of invites confrontation sometimes, whether we are out playing frat boys for shit beer pitchers or dining on a patio. She is very likely to talk trash if she sees something that displeases her. She's a rich kid from the Bay Area but doesn't come off spoiled. Actually, she is overly generous. She supports Brandon, who is a pro skater that doesn't pull in a tremendous amount of money. He's my friend from Isla Vista and a skate hero of the whole city, a role that doesn't pay as much as you might think.

Sarah is a statuesque beauty whose lineage hails from the barbaric tribes of Germany. A dozen or so generations of better and better health care and less of a need to ravage villages have turned her bloodline pretty. A vertically long face with sullen, ice-blue eyes, and ample lashes that swish you into her agenda. She wears straight brown hair to the nape of her neck and Oshkosh overalls. She also runs racks of pool balls and might just kick you in yours if you give her any lip. She can commonly be found at the pool tables amongst a bunch of visor wearing snapper heads, laying down lessons from the tip of her stick. She lets them know, "I'll wait to break until you get back with that pitcher of beer you just lost. Don't dilly dally now, Chet. Is that your name? Chet? Ha-ha, I bet your name's Chet. Hurry back, and you can Chet me out as I leave you with seven balls on the table again. Ha-ha. Fuckin' Chet, man. What a fucking clown. Budweiser, Chet! None of that Meister-Brau shit!"

Sarah sure does look off-balance the day my probation officer shows up with a drug-sniffing police dog, though. Next thing you know, they're out in the backyard, and this fuckin' dog is jumping up and down prancing through Sarah's pot plants while I shit in my pants. This dog is stupid, though. The only signal it gives is that it's having the time of its life, gayly fluttering about the felony herbs. Perhaps because they aren't budding yet, and they look more like tomato plants? Or that I deserve a break for once? At any rate, I don't go to jail today.

After I piss in a cup for Officer Wiersema to take on the road, we're all alone. I give Sarah a look of murder, and she says, "Fine, I'll get rid of them." Then she rethinks it, "Well, next time they come, shouldn't everything look the same? Won't they get suspicious if things are different?"

I'm not having it, "You mean when those plants are two-feet taller, and sticky purple buds are poppin' out everywhere? Move them little doggies out, Sarah!!"

Other than that, things go on without much event besides me failing to achieve gainful employment. Things start getting tense around the house. I'm short on the rent, and Sarah isn't giving any clues she's going to cover me. She's already supporting Brandon. Shawna is a dry well because that t-shirt investment was student loan money. That is a debt you can't get rid of, and the interest accumulates exponentially. It seems like this fact is something she hadn't considered before now. It's becoming a real wedge issue.

She gives me the keys to her stepdad's black '72 Chevelle as a last-ditch effort, hoping maybe I'll drive around looking for a job. Instead, I go pick up Frankie Hill, Kit Erickson, and Seth Napel.

We go joyriding and almost crash into an old lady in the Goleta K-mart parking lot. I have never driven before and have no license. The way she just casually tosses me the keys convinces me that I can drive well, that I didn't even need practice. This confidence leads me to drive in a stress-free and spontaneous manner that ends in nothing terrible. I even get the fucker up to 110 on Ward Memorial Freeway before the hood starts shaking.

It's also possible she is trying to get me thrown in jail for driving without a license as a dramatic form of divorce. Indeed, a beanie-wearing hoodlum with made up driving rules, tearing along in a Chevelle with Harley Davidson stickers on the back, should raise a few red flags with the overly eager local police. However, Lady Luck is on my side this week. Shawna will have to be less creative and more conventional to get rid of me if, indeed, this is her plan.

Black Sabbath

I'm offered a bit of respite from my brewing troubles in the form of a Black Sabbath concert. Heroin Dan has an extra ticket, and he picks me up on the corner of Santa Barbara Street and De La Guerra by the True Grit denim store. Just like that, we are on the 101 South in his rickety VW Van that sounds like rabbit farts escaping through ripped tracing paper. We make a few pit stops on Olympic Boulevard in Los Angeles to pick up the things Dan will need to enjoy a rock concert. On one corner, we get some crack. The next block, a crack pipe.

At our last visit, we stop on an uphill facing block. An old Mexican man comes out, looking up and down the street, now focusing on us to gauge if we are cops or not. He takes one look at the crosshatched razorblade cuts on Heroin Dan's forearms and his giant, warped, melonesque head of heroinality, and his face changes from suspicious to a big hospitable smile. He unprofessionally blurts out, "Whatchu need!?"

"Eight," Dan anxiously replies, checking the rearview. It's the first time I've ever seen him be careful about anything, anything at all.

The old man whistles up to the porch, and out trots who I'm guessing is his pre-teen granddaughter.

"Ocho," he says to her. And one by one, she vomits up eight heroin balloons.

"*Bluuuht...blaahrf,*" six more of those and we're off.

Up to this point, I feel I have seen and done a lot of shit in my young life. But I gotta say, my brain is pretty fucked up right now. I look over at Dan, and he's looking out the windshield, his eyes bugged out, rocking back and forth in his spring squealing captain's chair.

"*City of Angellllls,*" he lovingly sings.

"That was fucked up, Dan, and I would appreciate it if we could get to the venue before I experience any more things that regular people would consider...disturbing."

My wish is not granted. Heroin Dan finds a parking spot a block outside the drug swap meet and proceeds to smoke a crack rock. Exhaling the genocidal cloud while his lower jaw spasms, he turns to me and says, "Better than coffee, you want some?"

"I'm good, Dan," I sigh, in acceptance that none of this is in my control anymore.

"You're missing out. It's just concentrated cocaine."

I mull it over. I reason that at least if I die, I can't get evicted. After a short contemplation, I decide this will *not* be the first time I smoke crack.

I want it to be classier.

We eventually arrive at the Pacific Coast Amphitheatre in Orange County. The openers are Sepultura, a Brazilian metal band that shreds hard, otherwise, they wouldn't be on tour with people like Tony Iommi, Ozzy Osborne, and Rob Halford, that's for fucking sure! For this reason, we only miss half their set. Second, on the roster is Black Sabbath. They have Judas Priest's frontman, one of the manliest homosexuals you will ever come across, Rob Halford, singing for them. This is the fucking middle band! Are you kidding me? Now you know why I risked my life to get here. And Ozzy is the headliner! When I showed up to the first day of fifth grade class wearing a Tijuana poncho, it was *these* bands whose concert pins adorned it in a lightning bolt pattern down each side of my chest, my blonde and unruly rocker mop causing Mrs. Ogilvie to take a step back in terror. I've been metal since the motherfuckin' jump, cousin!

And get this, it's the last show of the tour, and everyone knows Ozzy is going to do some songs at the end with his old band, Black Sabbath, for the first time in over a decade! Siiiiiick! Everyone thinks they know, but still. Just the prospect of that, as a possibility?? I would have driven down here with six Heroin Dans, all of us crammed into a clown car.

We start navigating the parking lot in our *Hey cops, search this!* van. There are cops with barking dogs everywhere. I don't know if you know this, but Orange County is a dick. It's all retired judges and asshole cops. So, think about what their reaction was when they saw **this** rock concert flyer? "Oh, it's **ON** devil worshippers," would be my educated guess.

People's spike-covered black leather jackets are getting rifled through by deputies. Their dogs are alerting that: *Yes! Drugs are nearby, and lots of them!* Others are getting the inside of their mouth's searched with flashlights.

It's fuckin' Dachau, man! I'm getting legit scared by what I see outside the window. I go to beg Dan to wait to start partying, but it's too late. He already has a brown lump in a spoon with a lighter underneath it, singing, *"A spoonful of sugaaar, helps the medicine go doooown."*

"What the fuck, Dan?!" as if I have a right to be surprised by anything at this point.

"You seem a little stressed out. You should smoke some of this," Dan offers in a helpful tone, like a satanic Mary Poppins subscribing some cough syrup to a raspy toddler.

I'm like, "You can smoke it?"

A piece of tinfoil is quickly produced as if Dan had it ready for the short window of time that he figured I'd be willing, disoriented, and stressed enough to take him up on his sordid offer. Next thing you know, I'm chasing the dragon, puffin' Dr. Pepper, wafting in *the problem*. That's right, I am smoking heroin for the first time. It's a day that has now stretched into **a night** of many firsts. Initially, the feeling is obscure. Soon, it feels like helium for the soul. By the fifth hit, I'm like, "Ohhh, now I get it." The reliable stress shakes in my hands dissipate immediately, and I'm floating on a fluffy jacuzzi cloud. Still, inside the van, we hear the first jagged riffs of Sepultura, which signals Dan is only going to take four or so more hits and injections of various drugs before he feels ready enough to leave his illicit cocoon. Personally? I feel fuckin' great!

After a bit, Dan jostles me out the door, and we're into the big show. We make it to the top of the enormous grass amphitheater and settle down. I start chugging $10 cups of Budweiser, and the show is just... gargantuan! This is the culmination of all that I have loved since I was nine years old, which is only slightly more than a decade ago, but so much has happened. Jesus Satan. So much.

Right here before me, performing in raucous, ear-shattering style, are my childhood heroes. Like if Hitler showed up at Ronald Reagan's 8th birthday party. How stoked would little Ronny have been, right? It's all too unbelievable. Heroin Dan came through, I gotta admit. Several of the greatest of the greats, playing right before me. Look at Ozzy, in his ironic halo of stage light and his unquestionable rock god invincibility. It's just as I imagined, yet could never possibly imagine. By the end, I'm ready to just be arrested and brought to the gates of hell for my many well-enjoyed sins of the day. So much metal.

Ozzy finishes without doing some of the central classics, and I start to get sick. I have to lay on my side. I didn't know that heroin and alcohol mixed together cause an allergic reaction. I'm glad the show is over. I made it to the end. Yes! But what about the encore? What about Ozzy getting back on stage with Black Sabbath for the first time since before I had hair on my nuts?

Then! Ozzy does come back out to the stage, and he says, "Hey, I know ye was expectin' something like this. And I'm gonna do it! I'm gonna do some old tunes with me old mates. Let's bring 'em back out! Black Saaabbath!"

What?! I can't see anything because I'm lying on my side, all sick. We're at the top of a giant grass hill in one of the very back rows. The posers in front of us are blocking my view. They don't deserve this like I do. I assume the band is not only in formation but have planned on starting right out the gate, while we're all still in complete awe. They then begin assaulting our mystified brains. Sure, we expected it, but now that it's happening, we're not sure what to do.

"Whaaaaaayyyyrrrroowww!!!! Whaaaaaayyyyyrrrrowwwww!!!!" What?! This song?! Oh…my…fuckin'…god!

And then, an epic thing happens. The heroin makes me puke up the beer and the girl on the blanket in front of me shrieks. She has to move as my dastardly vomit gains downhill momentum, ruining all before it! This gives me a view of the greatest rock and roll band of all time, playing the greatest rock song of all time: "War Pigs."

"Generals gathered in their MASSSESSSSSS!!! Just like witches at BLACK MASSESSS!!!!! Evil minds that plot destructionnnn!!!! Sorcererrrrs of death's constructionnnnnn!!!"

The Downward Spiral

A week later. I'm still jobless. I can feel the last of the love my girlfriend has for me flickering out. I withdraw into Sega Golf in preemptive grief. A few weeks later, after some all-time shouting matches, one of which ends with her sister pulling some scissors on me, my first girlfriend tosses me to the curb. I'm in shock, and I call her from payphones drunk and crying. She doesn't yield. These are dark times.

I quickly become a dive bar champion. Any place with dollar drinks or 50-cent taco happy hours should be afraid. Alex's Cantina and El Paseo restaurants, the Mad Cat, Side Pocket, Mel's, Zelo, Soho, and Toe's Tavern? I would like to thank you for the patience you are about to be required to have with me during this rough time in my life. The Sportsman Bar? Fuck you. I don't take any of that shit back.

One of the low points that come quite early after being tossed back into the *couch surf circuit* is making the mistake of mixing GHB with too much alcohol. Some motherfucker with a gallon jug full of the stuff at the party says, "It's just some natural amino acids bro, kind of like a light ecstasy high."

That shit fucks me up.

I wake up in a rose bush of all things with scratches on my forearms, and all I remember is puking until I dry heaved. After an hour of that, I thought my stomach was going to flip inside out and start playing a bagpipe version of Danny Boy. I probably sought out this hellish thorny protection because I knew I was about to pass out, defenseless. My wallet is still there, just as empty as when my internal lights went. At least I didn't get picked clean like a Civil War soldier, dead on the field of Antietam.

I had finally slept due to being in a completely prone position. The last mouthful of puke, hidden from the dry heaves until after I pass out, finally burps up and sits in my cheek all night as I lay in the dirt. The little humdinger in the back of my throat just sat in that foul pool of acid all night frying like a tiny bratwurst. Two days later, I will cough off the tip of it into my hand, and over the next month or two, it grows back like a lizard's tail.

Uncle Jupiter

A month or so later, I'm still living the gutter life. I find myself standing outside of Mel's Bar with Jason, a guy that used to sing in some terrible band I saw a few times. A guy I would never see again after this day, but who I am best friends with now, waiting for the bar to open at 6 am.

It's us and some WW2 veteran hat-wearing regulars. They are here every morning and will slowly sip their Smirnoff's and their Old Grandad's on the rocks throughout the day. The bartenders pour generously for their service, and so their hands don't shake too badly. Mine are shaking moderately, as usual. Why? I don't know. Solitary confinement PTSD?

There are a couple of guys here that I sense aren't from around here, and judging from their behavior, they are so fresh out of prison, so they might even still have the gate money they give you when you get out. You get about $100 for every year they stole from you. One of them is staring at me, and since that is a *prison no-no*, I figure I should respond in terms he can understand. "You keep staring at me? You're going to watch me kill you, boy." I say to him, with an artificial Southern drawl. I lifted this line from a movie, but it's early, and I am behind on drinks, so original material might be hard to come by at the moment.

The guy just smiles at me in a sadistic grin and shakes his head up and down, like he likes it. So, you're a crazy motherfucker too, huh? I think. Maybe I'll sell him some coke later.

We finally get in there. Sunny, a middle-aged Hawaiian lady, isn't bartending, unfortunately. She's the greatest and seems to be the most tolerant of my *jackassery*, provided I do a little phony flirting. I put some Rolling Stones on the jukebox so that none of these assholes puts on Sinatra. Everyone loves the Stones, right?

We start playing pool with these guys. It turns out that "Yes," they did just get out of jail.

I find out they have some money. Enough to go to the Motel-6 and do a bunch of blow that I have Cisco deliver in his big white Cadillac. This money will represent six months from each of these guys' lives that the state was willing to compensate them for. I suppose I will hand them the rolled-up five-dollar bill first, out of respect for this sad fact.

Cisco is a large man with Jesus' folded praying hands tattooed on his neck and crazy glassed over eyes that I really should be more afraid of. This criminal codger with the money is scared I'm going to roll him, so I have to annoy Cisco by bringing him in the Cadillac. "Whoa, who is this guy?"

After a few cocktails, my wit has returned. "My uncle died; this is myother uncle here for the funeral"—this is a handy story I will use throughout the day.

Cisco buys it or maybe doesn't care. "Oh, I'm sorry. That's rough.

I got some good stuff for you guys. Gonna take all the sadness away. Cry later, eh."

"Thanks, Cisco. It's been a long week."

This last part, technically, isn't a lie.

Now we are at the Motel-6. One of these guys is super quiet, even after some lines. His buddy, my newfound uncle, takes a footlong blaster off the top of the TV. After a few minutes, he's out in the parking lot doing imaginary snow angels on a hood of the type of sedan you would expect to find in a Motel-6 parking lot. "I am a Roman Emperor! A Roman HOLY Emperor!" he cries.

We're watching the show from the balcony and laughing. The poor Asian family working the hotel comes out. It's the type of rundown hotel that's run by a first-gen and second-gen immigrant family, where the kids can't wait to get their business degree and get far away. A lady appearing to be the mother with big hair and bags under her eyes approaches, as the son hangs behind in the office doorway, hoping he doesn't have to get involved. "Wha's a-goin' onnnn heeeyah!" she scolds.

I shift quickly to a grave tone. "My uncle is upset because his brother died. He'll be asleep soon. They were very close. I'm sorry, you guys. We'll leave an extra tip on the dresser."

It's 9 am and much too early for this insanity. I'm sure we won't pull it off without the cops raiding the place. We start dragging The Emperor back up to the room, and the Asian lady, who is honestly sympathetic, says, "You want exra peerows?"

"Oh no, that's all right," I say with a sad, crackly voice.

The last thing we want is them seeing that all the flat surfaces in the room already look like a small snowstorm has dusted them.

Jason and I get this guy back up to the room, and we each do another fat bump, pinch half and leave the poor mute guy to try and handle Caligula junior here. As we leave the parking lot, we see the nice Asian lady coming out with a few pillows. We walk away a bit faster.

Keep Spiraling Bitch

After ten years, I find my friend Banks has returned from living in Amsterdam. All he did was party, become a Chomsky spouting lefty, and a pretty decent pool hustler. Pretty awesome. Soon we are taking over the pool table at the Mad Cat, winning more drinks than we need, and I'm trying to reinvent myself as a coke, weed, and ecstasy dealer. The area is crawling with other dealers, but my near-decade of experience selling pot in Isla Vista proves to have useful relevance. The problem is I'm on this rowdy streak because my heart is smashed to pieces. I'm trying to get thrown in prison or something equally disastrous, to show my ex-girlfriend what a big mistake she made. I'm doing a bang-up job so far. I bet she's about to take me back any minute.

I've already been kicked out of the Mad Cat three times, but the big softie that works the door keeps letting me in. Tonight, however, he has made a poor choice. Some shit bag wants to fight because he insists he had his quarters next, and we know that's not the case. I also suspect he's another dealer vying for the happy hour crowd's business here. He's a stocky little fucker, but he's exactly that: little. I shove him to see how interested he is in playing a stupid game of pool. He pops back up into my chest surprisingly quick and pushes me back a step. *Shit.* Now I'm going to have to go *full ass-kick* and risk a permanent ban, the dreaded 86.

I crack him in the head, and the bouncers are on us. We all end up outside where the battle continues. Banks decides to take this stocky little chump's charge, and I've got to give it to the little fucker, he has skills. Next thing you know, Banks' eye is gushing blood. It's as if time slowed down, and the little leprechaun whooshed up into the sky on a cushion of air to bring down a Goliath. Banks is 6'2" with a big barrel chest and gorilla arms, which are, apparently, strictly for show. He looks like a Chris Isaac-y Elvis. The girls love him, and now the ones smoking out front are going "Awwwww," while his eye bleeds all over the pavement.

I turn to defend my friend's bruised honor. The leprechaun tries his leap move redundantly and gets swatted down hard from the air like a tennis ball made of shit. He gets up slowly, and the bouncer comes charging up, yelling, "You guys need to take it down the block!" It's true, we're right in front of the bar's window. People inside are filling it up with the usual maniacal grins, excited shouting, and finger-pointing.

The leprechaun decides it isn't over and tries to get around the bouncer, who then grabs the guy like a hog at a fair. The front of him is sticking out between the bouncer's huge arm and his hip, providing me with a convenient opportunity to try and punch this little fucker's gold coins out of his pockets. *Whap!* He flies out the back of his temporary flesh manacle and hits the ground once again.

I guess he wasn't so great at fighting, after all, Banks just sucks at it. Great guy, though. Not much help in the bar brawls, but he pulls his weight as a chick magnet. The prettiest girl in the room always has friends that are almost as cute as her. I let Banks have the high maintenance chicks, and I scoop up the cuties with reasonable expectations. It's a perfect situation. I start backing away and make eye contact with the bouncer, winking in a *thanks for the assist* type way. We walk away, me cradling Banks' head and getting my only good shirt ruined with its blood.

Later that night, we go to Dead Ted's house to crash. Dead Ted is cool, and he doesn't care if people crash on the couch on occasion, provided you aren't too big a drain on the pad. He likes the company if you can make him laugh, and you're willing to help out a little.

They call him Dead Ted because he has a disease that was supposed to kill him by the time he was eight, then again at 12, then again and again and again. And he's still fuckin' here, almost thirty, laughing and spitting into the reaper's face. I guess I would be laughing a little bit too. He's a happy guy with an easy laugh. Everybody loves him, and no one feels sorry for him. Why? First of all, he won't allow it. Second, his vibe puts you past that.

He has Fredrickson's Disease, a degenerative, incurable *shit show* that slowly dissolves your spine and brain starting from the time you're a child. And they say there's a god. If there is, I would like to prison rape him someday. Despite Ted's spine sluggishly turning into a smoothie in front of us, the guy loves to have a good time. Sometimes—you didn't hear it from me—there's even known to be a bit of a rager at Dead Ted's house.

Ted's pad gets pretty wild. He's a skinny blonde kid with a big nose and an even bigger smile, kind of like a less sharply featured Beck, but with a touch of the Spina Bifida. He'll prop himself up and rock his head, smiling as ridiculous mayhem unfolds around him.

When I wake up super hungover on his couch, I know I can just go and rap with him for a bit. His laughs and complete lack of self-pity will inflate me a little bit. Any problems that I may currently have seem like little whiny bitch complaints—way railer in comparison to what Ted's been through—and he's laughing all the time. "Shut up pussy," I say to myself in Ted's bathroom mirror after taking a little gutter urchin shower in the sink beneath it, being careful to leave little evidence I was here. Then I go out to headline for an audience of one again.

The only problem with Ted's house is this new asshole has moved in. You know? The guy that stopped going to karate class once he got the first belt and is now getting Chinese letters tattooed everywhere? 24 accessories on his shitty mountain bike? This newest transformation of his was curated after no one in town would let him be the D&D Dungeon Master anymore. Apparently, he was too cruel at it. You know the fucker I'm talking about. Every town has one. Maybe he didn't go into karate; perhaps he's one of your town's cops or doormen. A nerdy bully that has to justify intellectually and explain to you why he's trying to bully you. And he's super creative about his reasons, so anytime he wants to, he can rain down on your parade, like piss dribbles in a sad clown's pants. Like, he's saving you from yourself by being a dick. *That* fucker.

Somehow this guy weaseled himself into Dead Ted's house because that would be the *instructive uncle nirvana* of his whole fucking life. Now, he's trying to implement a: <u>No one can crash on the couch more than once a week unless they're going to drink and drive rule.</u> What the fuck? That's classist. You have to own a car to sleep here? Fuck that. A few years ago, he was the same angry roommate that hated the couch crashers at a different pad I hung out at. It's a small town, and this guy is starting to cramp my style. Fuck this guy. We are going to war. I think *he* knows that *I* know he's probably only a yellow belt. He's scared I might pop him in the nose and blow his scam that no one believes anyway.

Banks and I find a six-pack in the fridge and drink it, promising each other to replace it tomorrow. Ted doesn't store much beer in the fridge, so we are assuming it belongs to Karate Boy. *Thop!* We pound the last bottles in the leftover sixer. Who the fuck goes to sleep with beer still left anyway? Appropriate punishment, in our opinion. Maybe we'll replace it, probably not.

Karate Boy probably hears Banks and me talking and laughing and understands the sound of his microbrew bottle caps getting popped off. Early in the morning, after he'd probably been steaming over us having eventful lives compared to his piss bottle of a soul and not having the guts to confront us personally, he sneaks out into the living room and pours water into the cable box. It is destroyed, and we have been successfully blamed. I know what that clever piece of shit did. We never broke shit at *our friend's* houses, just *everybody else's.* He had been ruminating on what he would do the next time our paths crossed, and he was ready. Touché motherfucker. Touché.

Now, in those days, cable is a relatively new, delicate, and expensive habit. The bill for that ruined cable box is $500. Fuck. Fuck you, Cox Cable. I'm sure the future board members of Comcast are studying your every move. So, even though I could have pleaded my case to Ted, I let it go. I accept temporary banishment, until two weekends from now. Nothing is more ruthless on the sneak than a coward that wants everyone to think his muscles aren't hollow gym balloons.

The next morning Banks says, "Oh shit, I want you to meet someone, let's go." So, we go to this bookstore and walk into the back, and there's a small table with an old guy I don't recognize. We wait in a short line and get up to the front, and I see that it's Ralph Nader, the future presidential candidate. The guy invented seat belts or something, and some will blame him for giving GW the presidency once Bill Clinton's time is up in a few years. Whether that's true or not, he is here in front of us now, gearing up for that, and ready to stir the youth into action.

About a dozen college students are milling around or getting books signed. Banks, left-wing scholar that he has become in his decade in Holland, has his book ready in hand to be signed by the understated and perpetually fatigued looking hero, Ralph Nader. He looks as rumpled as his suit. I get up in line after Banks, no book in hand. Ralph looks at me, gives a lazy smile, and asks, "What brings you here today?"

I try to think of something funny to say to this Bernie Sander's long-lost brother, type. After a moment of consideration, I come up with, "Well, I'm trying to get young people interested in activism, I guess."

"Well, that's great. Are you in college?"

"Nope," I say.

"Well, what organization are you a part of?" Ralph asks.

"Mostly bottles and spray paint so far," I say.

Ralph looks a little confused but still engaging. "Well, I wish you luck, young man. Remember, peace is the answer."

"I'm not so sure about that, Ralph, but I wish you luck as well." We shake on it.

As we are walking out into the parking lot, Banks says, "You're a jack ass, Scales."

"Seems pretty stupid to take any of this shit seriously, doesn't it? It's not like we have any kids that we know of. Loosen up, man. The apocalypse is nigh, and it's not of our choice or helping," says the punk rock Nihilist in me. The stoner-surfer-hippy must be napping off in the dunes somewhere, unperturbed.

The ever-patient Banks sighs, with a concealed smile escaping at the last second. He won't loosen up; he cares about the world as much as I pretend not to.

"We have to try to make this horror show of a planet better than we found it. We are grown men now. It's up to us. Everything Ralph says is right, and I am not just going to hope he's the next president. I'm going to try and make it so; however, I can."

"If you like him, I like him, Banks."

Banks smiles at this and figures that's as much as he will get for now. He'll keep needling everybody. It's ok if it takes time, that's how civic discourse works.

Broken Doomsday Clock

Things go on like this for a bit. It turns out my bottom has no limit. I raw dog bar skanks in bathrooms, challenging both the reaper and my probation officer at every turn. I am on informal probation now. I only have to go into appointments every month or two and lie my ass off that the shirt business is doing great. Act *not crazy* for a few minutes. Easy-peasy, right?

For money, I've started dabbling, albeit with hesitation, in selling blow. The judge only said not to sell weed, right? People downtown have endless amounts of money to spend on cocaine. The shit practically sells itself. I start sniffing it regularly to make the empty douche bags I'm talking to sound appealing. The coke scene is weak, but I need the money to get out of the *couch surf circuit.*

I never really did cocaine in Isla Vista. I was always broke, and everyone knew it, so it's not like I was going to kick in the locked bathroom doors to get it. I never really hung out with someone if they seemed too coked out—too many long stories with no tie up at the end. But now because I'm selling the shit, these people are *all* I'm around.

You know most bartenders get drunk most of their shifts, right? It starts because that's the only way to deal with all the drunks every night. You have to be drunk too—the same with dealing blow. First, you do it just to deal with the fucking blabber mouths you meet. Soon, you begin to need it. Shit sneaks up on you. You feel like it was sudden, but it took a year.

A cokehead is a bad thing to be, kids. Some people can cruise to the bar, have a few light beers, watch the band, go home, smoke a joint, and fuck. I was never like that. I become a terrible monster who makes too much of a habit out of shooting my own foot and stabby-stabbin' myself between the shoulder blades.

1995 is one of my bad years. Just after Kurt Cobain decides to check out "allegedly." Mike Tyson retires with 44 knockouts, and OJ is found not guilty. I am sure the verdict comes in after a secret cash drop to Judge Ito is made, saving Compton's liquor stores from being torched again. The Rodney King Riots were just a few years ago, and LA is still scared of the potential sequel that this case has presented.

Hip-hop hasn't douched out on bling, cognac, and stripper videos yet. Also, it's finally knocked rock and roll into second place on the jukeboxes. The first time rock and roll hasn't been in the top spot since the polka era. Guitar snobs everywhere are shocked and destroyed. Rap has been enjoying a long, socially conscious golden age that started almost a decade ago with KRS-1 and Public Enemy. It is now being led by greats such as the not long to live, Tupac Shakur, the immortal Tribe Called Quest, and TheRoots. Nas' Illmatic is still in heavy rotation at house parties. For variety, you have the dudes in Wu-Tang releasing good solo shit, and unserious, dirty, and mischievous stuff like Too Short and Cypress Hill. Snoop Dog became an instant legend two years ago with his debut album, Doggy Style, which is still getting more play than a pre-plastic surgery, Mickey Rourke, in an Ohio strip club.

Rap has grown up. Now, 20 years since its first inklings in Queens, you can't say it's not real, or that it's just a fad anymore. It is here to stay, and the establishment is traumatized by that. All this makes me a fan, though I have trouble wrapping my brain around it sometimes. I always just thought it would be rock and roll that called the kids to the fight. The more, the merrier, I guess.

And what a time for this newest of major music genres to beat its chest in blossomed adulthood. Puffy hasn't ruined it all with snifters of Hennessy and fur coats yet. White kids are co-opting black culture like it's the English stealing the blues again. Rap isn't as easy to mimic as the blues, however, and the rich town cracker teens of America will have to just settle for the fashion, slang, and this new dude, Eminem. People that used to say, "Rad grind, brah," are now saying, "that was the shiznit," "mad props," "so phat," "super blingy." Girls named Becky are wearing baggy Dickies and crooked baseball hats. People are even trying to spit weak freestyle.

It has been a crazy, fucked up year where it feels like the nuclear clock is about to ring midnight, but rap has made us fearless. We're ready to pull our sonic straps on all this ridiculous shit. My brain can only try to catch up, but I know I love it. Times are changing fast, people are starting to high-five my AC/DC tank top ironically. Am I a dinosaur at 23? The jukeboxes and house parties play all this shit until the records wear out, along with Weezer, Smashing Pumpkins, Rage Against the Machine, and let's never forget the ever-present and *way played out*: Sublime. Ace Ventura and Braveheart are the movies to sneak into stoned. Someone had to tell me Braveheart was a history flick; I wanted it to be last week. Too much is happening too fast.

1995 is a crazy ass year for the whole world, not just my little scene. Timothy McVeigh bombs the shit out of the Oklahoma Federal building with goddamn fertilizer, the Prime Minister of Israel gets his ass assassinated, and Sarin gas is used on a Japanese subway.

Crazy shit, man.

Teen Sperm and Rugburn

In the summer, half the apartments are traditionally vacant in Isla Vista because all the college kids leave. I go out there sometimes. Having been gone a few years, I'm not in the scene anymore. The town is half empty anyway, which suits me. I'm in the party loop downtown, so I have to dedicate most of my time there, but it's nice to come out here sometimes and rest along the cliffs overlooking the ocean. Try and sort it all out. It's mostly great to not see any of the coke heads I now consort with for a while.

In Santa Barbara dive bars, almost any customer will pay full retail for midgrade coke all night long and then some. You actually have to turn your flip phone off when you go to sleep because the pieces of shit will repeatedly call you until you pick up. "You got any? You got any coke, man!?" Shiva help you if they know which window you sleep behind, they'll be rap-tap-tappin' at it like a pilled-up Poe Raven.

It's nice to turn off my phone, come out to the old neighborhood and relax. One such night we are up on a roof, drinking beers, smoking weed, and looking out at the ocean about a 100-feet down. Everything is mellow.

There are about eight of us and people start pairing off. It's summer, and we're horny in the warm Santa Ana winds that are whipping up and over the Santa Barbara mountains.

I didn't grieve my first exploded love relationship very long. The night before, I broke my newly single cherry on a 19yo with a scorpion tramp stamp and wild stories about how she robbed a bank when she was 17. After seeing how degraded she was, I believed her. She totally shotgun robbed my remaining boyhood virtue. Pretty sure Pot Plant Sarah goes straight to Shawna with this information. We were all playing pool at Déjà Vu together last night when it all went down. Sarah saw enough to put six and nine together and most likely spread the news as quick as Rosemary was spreading her ass cheeks, revealing the unsatisfiable, *rusty sheriff's badge of courage*. The progress I had been making was gone the next time I *crybaby bitch* call Shawna. The tryst before us now promises to be slightly sweeter in nature, barely:

A girl from the high school I barely went to has grown up into a bit of a looker, and she's giving me the moo-moo eyes. Someone has a boombox, and we are listening to Minor Threat, The Misfits, Bad Religion, and Blind Melon for variety. The warm winds combine with our copious young lust and is making the electric charges between our bodies palpable. I work up the guts and go up to the tall skinny girl named Danica and give her a kiss. She seems nervous, and we slide our tongues in and out of each other's mouths like hummingbirds at a feeder. "Do you have a condom? Can we go to your place?" she asks me. *My place?* No wonder this is going well, she is unaware of my living situation.

"I know a place close by," I say, leaving it at that.

And I do. Last night I broke into a vacant apartment a block away with the bank robber/sex addict. Soon, we arrive, I slide the side window open and hold her hand as she lifts her leg up and over the threshold. The only items in the apartment are some clothing, an empty set of Mickey's Big Mouth beer bottles, and a used condom from last night. This is about the time she realizes there won't be a California king of any sort in her near future.

I get off her shirt, and we go at it. She seems to be self-conscious of her little plum-sized titties, so I lick them and suck them like they're from the Best of Playboy. And for me, they are. So soft and with rosy pink nipples hardening as a strong hint to me that they like it. About to sever an artery on my zipper, I rip off both our pants right there on the carpet. I struggle to get at her pussy like it's the last can of SpaghettiOs in the zombocalypse. I know her *Purse of the Lucky Pickle* is as excited as her nipples because I can faintly smell it priming itself in the dark. I follow the light trail of flowers and Ahi and lick her love bump through her underwear. I get those worked over to the side and start flicking her wet *man in the boat* with my forefinger, frantically ringing the *devil's doorbell*. After thirty seconds, she's starting to moan. "Where's the condom?" she asks.

Shit. I used the only one last night. "Ok, I'll get it. I gotta go to the bathroom anyways."

I go in there, take an eternal beer piss, simultaneously searching for the used rubber from last night. There it is, draped over the sink where I flung it just 24 hours ago. I rinse it out and give it a look. As long as she's wet enough, it shouldn't matter that the little drop of lube they put on the tip is long gone. I palm it guiltily and head back out.

We start going at it again, and I'm playing her pussy with my fingers like a methed-out Keith Richards on his last unbroken guitar string. I figure it's juicy enough, and I'm hard as shit because I know I'm about to be inside a cute brunette. I almost tear the rubber trying to get it on my dick, and I thrust it into her squishy meat wallet before she figures out I'm using the worst version of birth control since the *pull-in* method. The *kundalini tango* has begun. I'm thrusting and pumping, going mad, no finesse, just a frantic race to the finish line. We moan and groan as I drill her midsection into the cheap carpet.

In the end, I roar, in window shaking finality, and we collapse in slumber, naked but for the jacket that had been under her ass. Now it's draped over our sweaty abdomens in an attempt to be a blanket.

We wake up early because that Isla Vista summer fog has rolled in at dawn and made it chilly. She looks through her sleepy eyes at the place I've brought her to and realizes this won't be a story she tells her grandchildren, not even her slutty best friend who saw us trail off last night. How much will this story have to be modified to make it acceptable to that judgmental slut? We quickly re-clothe ourselves and go off to a payphone so she can call her mother to come pick her up. It is insinuated that I will wait until the car is in sight before I can be done with the situation. We are sitting there, drinking coffee from Styrofoam cups, waiting, and she says, "My back itches, is there a bug bite or something?"

She lifts her shirt, and I am horrified at what I see. "Oh shit!"

The jacket had slipped out from under her, and now she has the worst case of rug-burn I have ever seen. There's a scab on her spine from the top of her butt-crack to her midback. "Uhm."

"What? What is it?" She tries to see her back and does a half-circle, like a dog chasing its tail.

I try to reassure, "Well, it looks like you have a little rug-burn from last night. It's going to scab up a little."

She looks sad that she's not going to walk away from last night unscathed. Her Mom pulls up, and she heads toward the car, slouching in shame. I stay where I am and wave. I decide that I can't tell anyone about this. Shit! They'll nickname her Spinal Tap!

My Sister and the
Guatemalan Civil War

And the hits just keep coming. My mother, the gypsy-blooded adventurer, thought it would be a good idea to enter Guatemala by sneaking over a fence. Apparently, she is unaware of their ongoing 35-year civil war that is supposedly simmering down. But is it? Is it really? Sources on the ground tell me that is bullshit, and by "on the ground," I mean my bleeding sister. She's hopped the northern Guatemalan border with my Mom in the night, which nobody does. At least not in that direction. Now she's walking around, a 6-foot tall blonde-haired American teenager in the middle of a war. A war between Mayan descendant rebels and Mayan descendants with some Spanish blood raped into them. For some reason, the latter think rape blood makes them superior to the Indians with less Spanish rape blood in them. Strange world we live in.

In 1960, the city elites in Guatemala were tired of hearing the Indians complain about their ancestral lands being desecrated. This is the year before the Bay of Pigs invasion, so things are agitated between the US and Cuba. A strategic country in which to launch attacks is perceived by the *bloodthirsty war hawks* in the Pentagon as critical. So, the CIA pulls out its tired, one-page playbook and installs a military dictator in Guatemala.

Fast forward 35 years, the country is still inflamed with chaos and Indian genocide. Kissinger would be very proud.

There are soldiers everywhere, and one of them—probably a teenager like my sister—tells her to stop, and she's like, "Fuck that," and starts running. He levels his rifle and *bam!* Just like that, fires a bullet into her leg, breaking the femur in a multitude of places. Let's just finish this story as an interview and let her tell it.

J.C.: "How old were you when you got shot in Guatemala?"

Hannah: "16."

J.C.: "I'm sorry I was in the bars getting drunk when I should have been doing a good job protecting you as your oldest brother. I just didn't know the extent of it until this event happened. Do you want to tell me the story?"

Hannah: "It was late at night. A car full of what looked like soldiers blocked our car, and we had to pull over. I saw a chance to escape, but the guy that was driving was forced into the back, and he sat on my dress, pinning me to my seat. The soldiers ordered us out. They were not too bright, but they knew we were not supposed to drive on the roads at night. Mom and I had no idea."

"They separated us, and I got a soldier assigned to me that was acting very strangely. I started to run away, but he caught up to me and shot my femur at close range. Probably so I wouldn't run. He threw a rope around my neck and dragged me along. He was looking for a tree to hang me but gave up. There was only a banana tree and a cornfield ahead of us. He left me to bleed to death. I started to feel my feet stiffen, so l took my boots off. I had seen pictures of soldiers in battle with their shoes off when they are dying. Maybe because when they are going into shock, it feels like their shoes are too tight."

"I crawled deeper into the cornfield. I felt very tired and peaceful. In a few minutes, maybe seconds, I saw my life flash before me like a movie. All the major things I had done. One thing stood out, I was mean to Mom. I made her life miserable, complained, and called her names when she didn't do anything. Suddenly, I heard her, and the couple call out to me. Oh, why don't they let me sleep? I knew I was dying, but I didn't care, it felt so good. Not long after, their voices woke me up, and ambulances arrived very quickly. The drivers made a joke that they were going to rape us."

"The hospital was big. It looked like they did experiments on the patients. One guy had what looked like a cage on his foot, holding his broken bones into place. It was fused with his flesh. When they gave me an X-ray, the machine was the size of the whole room. Is this thing going to give me cancer someday?"

"I was in the hospital for a few days, or maybe it was a week. The day I left, two female nurses and a male nurse put me in a full-body cast. The women seemed so scared of me getting raped they would barely let him help, and they wrapped me up so tight I couldn't go number two. The wrap got filled with pee. We eventually took the thing off."

"During my stay, they wanted to operate on me and put metal in there to keep my bones together. They kept coming to my room to try and pressure us into the free surgery. We refused, even though the American embassy told us we should do what the doctors want. I'm perfectly fine now."

"Whenever Mom was asleep, the nurse that worked closely with the doctor would come in and stab a needle into my arm. It hurt every time she did it. 'Your fuckin' mom, your fuckin' mom,' she would repeat."

"She didn't like that Mom was consulting with a natural doctor that said my bones could heal naturally. Then they took us to a smaller clinic that had a tin roof. It was so hot in there, and the babies cried all night long. It made me sad. I felt like crying for them. I left out that the soldier was trying to knock me out after the shooting, but he gave up after hitting me multiple times. I remember saying to myself, 'I ain't going down!' He kept staring at his hands real weird, holding them up. That's why I thought he was on drugs."

"The staff at the clinic proudly showed me two of the soldiers that had attacked us. They were outside on a steel table, dead with several bullet wounds. They carelessly lay on top of each other. They had lost so much blood that there was a trail of big clots. I didn't care either way. I had the worst pounding headache from all the blows I received, and my leg was swollen three times its normal size. My body was so stressed I could no longer pee on my own, so they put a catheter in for a few days. This was the most painful thing ever. When they took it out, a piece of my flesh and blood came out with the hose. I don't know, maybe they put it in wrong; maybe it's just like that."

"We stayed with a Guatemalan family for a month. Mom didn't call you guys or couldn't. She took me to a healer in Tapaculo, and l bathed in a hot water source in the mountains. Like a natural Jacuzzi. I don't remember what they're called."

J.C.: "Mom said she broke you out of one of those places by pushing you out of there on the wheeled hospital bed, got you into a truck taxi, and told him to get out of there quick!"

Hannah: "Probably the big creepy hospital because I remember her getting a cab quickly. They were always yelling at her there. Hey, you should put this in your book!"

J.C.: "That's a great idea. Ok, well, I'm putting it in just how you wrote it. I'm sorry again I wasn't able to save you from any of our family's struggles. You definitely had it the worst of all of us. Such a shame, but you still have a vibrance and positivity about you."

Hannah: "I believe in destiny. We wrote how our lives are supposed to be before we came here. We pick our parents and siblings, even our own names. I guess I'm too positive."

PS—Hannah's leg healed up with no surgery. She can run and skip with no sign of the injury. Just the knowledge there's a piece of lead floating around in there somewhere. Eventually, they make it back up through Guatemala and Mexico riding in pick-up trucks and third-class busses. The doctors in America said she would walk with a cane forever if they didn't rebreak the bone and put a bunch of screws and plates in her femur. My mother said, "No." Instead, she just prayed over that leg tirelessly, foraging in fields for comfrey leaves and wrapping them around Hannah's leg.

Against all the odds, she healed back to 100%. I'm not saying doctors are always full of shit, but they can be condescendingly confident that they are right when they're not. If they fuck you up, they will forget it in a week, but you'll be screwed forever. All because you were convinced by their certainty and $20 words. Walk into a hospital only in cases of emergency, my friends, and with a grain of suspicion. A notebook full of questions probably wouldn't hurt either. 50% of people die from the chemo, not the cancer, that's all I'm saying. Chinese herbs and hippy cures for preventative medicine, and hopefully, you never have to go into a filthy hospital except to see your baby born, if even then.

Also, fuck the United States Government for causing the shitty *domino effect* in Guatemala that got my sister shot. You are the biggest asshole this world has ever seen.

GWAR

What the fuck? I find myself asking myself this more than twice before the metal band GWAR starts their fourth song. What a bizarre, otherworldly spectacle. Frank Frazetta on Mars, Salvador Dali meets Conan the Barbarian.

I knew about this band and had heard about all their insane theatrics, but nothing can prepare you. It's fuckin' awesome! A seven-foot puppet of Ronald Reagan comes out and starts wagging his judgmental finger at the audience, who responds with a beer into his stupid face. Next thing you know, an even bigger puppet of the Pope comes strutting out and bends Ronnie over and starts butt fucking him until he squeals. All the while, a band dressed like Mad Max strippers play the heavy metal of Hades.

Between NBA player sized puppet rapings, the band grinds out the thematic metal opera that is Ragnarök. A tale of the end of the world. Our players, Oderus Urungus, and his sister, Sylmenstra, have been kidnapped and forced to mate by space aliens to bear an evil, intergalactic, sacrificial baby.

This play / album has a sub-theme that unfolds with each song. The world is going nuts, simultaneously afflicted with a sex plague and an asteroid hurtling directly towards earth, giving the youth no reason to not just fuck everything up. The story takes an anti-Christianity turn as it is revealed that the asteroid is actually a colossal robot, warrior pope, here to punish the wicked youth for having fun.

Between songs, a giant Jerry Garcia comes out and tries to play a guest set. The singer and mastermind of GWAR, Oderus Urungus, doesn't take kindly to that. He proceeds to walk over with his giant demon face and three-foot shoulder spikes jutting out of his oversized battle armor and rips off Jerry Garcia's idiotic puppet head. A three-inch-wide spurt of blood starts gushing onto the audience; gallons upon gallons of Jerry Garcia's sweet, syrupy hippy blood soaking all of our faces and the floor. The pit becomes more of a slip and slide of death than a hurricane of pain.

The audience goes nuts as the band grinds out tune after tune of their Valhalla sci-fi metal. The mangy audience thrashes about with huge pupils and wet, bloody shirts. There is nothing quite like a GWAR show. Afterwards, I rush a few blocks over from The Underground to Toe's Tavern to catch the last song or two of Ugly Kid Joe.

Now look, I am not a hater of Ugly Kid Joe's music like all the other hard rockers in Santa Barbara. They're probably jealous of who is getting all the pussy. As a person who may be a little snobby in *his own* rock and roll choices, let's just say the adage *if you can't beat 'em, join 'em,* makes a lot of sense to me in this particular situation. Of course, hard rockers would never accept jokey pop-metal, right? Dumb asses. Jokey pop-punk, like NOFX and Lagwagon? Fine. But don't try to be metaling it out. So dumb. The guys in Ugly Kid Joe are fantastic dudes. Klaus Eichstadt? The guitar player? Nicest guy you could ever meet, totally unassuming, humble, and funny as fuck. What's to hate? The singer, Whitfield Crane? He might be the funnest guy to party with ever. A real party Svengali that won't leave you too hurt in the morning unless you're a beach bikini girl's heart. He is generous as hell and always has a big smile between the entirety of his wideset jaw. Long haired rockers who like to get the ladies in a good mood for the after-parties. Plus, their fans buy a bunch of weed and other stuff from me. Nothing but love from me, babies! Unfortunately, your biggest hit is your most annoying song, but you can say that happened to a lot of bands. What can I say? The public is an idiot. Look at the politicians they elect.

After they finish playing and everyone has been hanging out for a while, some guys come up to us and introduce themselves as GWAR! They had taken off their outfits and come in regular stuff so you couldn't recognize them. How about that, haters? GWAR came to see Ugly Kid Joe after playing their own headline, full theatre set.

Soon, half of GWAR, Whitfield, and I are all at Whitfield's blue Pontiac GTO, pulling out a shit ton of fireworks from the trunk to go light at the beach. As we're standing there, a street dealer from the intersection of Garden and Haley has made his way over. He says the heat is on over there at the moment.

"Fuck it," I say and buy a 20 rock off him. A second later, some cops drive by us. They have subconsciously smelled out where the most concentrated area of felonies is being committed.

"What the fuck is going on here?" they say.

Before they even get out of the car, Whitfield goes up to them and plays some Jedi mind trick shit. I am ready to run if they get out of their vehicle, but they don't.

"Put those fireworks back in the trunk, and **do not** drive away from here," they say in a fatherly tone.

Then they leave. Sometimes cops are just too lazy to do paperwork, but this is inexplicable. The missed opportunity of being able to say you arrested GWAR, the singer of Ugly Kid Joe, and to be able to slap a prison inducing crack cocaine charge on J.C. Scales, aka 'the town's main problem?' So many people from so many different locales and walks of life would instantly come together to worship you forever. And these dumb rich town cops blow it. They could have quit the department and done speaking tours where the audiences throw roses onto the stage. Fuckin' suckers.

Ten minutes later, we are driving, 'away from here,' in Whit's Pontiac, which we weren't going to do in the first place, but now we figure we should clear the area.

20 minutes later, we are lighting off all the fireworks outside GWAR's tour bus in Carpinteria's Motel-6 parking lot. I'm creating my personal trail of cocaine-fueled pyrotechnic chaos through the Motel-6 parking lots of California. I could care less if they try and ban me from the entire chain.

After the last rocket lights up the sky, we are inside their tour bus, and I'm trying to divide up a single crack rock six ways so we can smoke it in a 7-Up can. Whitfield, the probable crack virgin, handles the can with his fingertips like its nitroglycerin or something. Not the emergency room clogging excess you'd imagine, but hey, I can say I've smoked crack with GWAR. Did *you* smoke crack with GWAR? Did you corrupt the frontman of the band who foisted "Everything About You" onto the undeserving public? Oh, you didn't?

After being gifted a laminated backstage pass to commemorate the occasion, Whitfield and I part with the band.

I wake up on his couch the next morning.

"Man, you're partying pretty hard these days aren't you, bro?" says a concerned Whitfield.

Now, when the singer of a rock band tells you that you're partying too hard, you might want to start analyzing some of your later in the day habits. And it's true, I used to rage with what I like to call a balance of chaos and *certain poetry*.

"J.C., I will give you $10,000 if you quit partying for a year. I'm worried about you. You think you could do it?" he offers in a brotherly tone.

"Fuck yeah!" I say excitedly because I've never had a shot at 10 Gs before. So, I take the offer, and I make it for about three months. Not of not partying, three months before he catches me drunk in a bar and disqualifies me.

The Broom Man

Santa Barbara collects and breeds its fair share of eclectic, bizarre, and unique individuals. An homage to them all would require a book of its own, but some are too magical not to mention. The Broom Man is an old, tall, skinny, highly dapper black man in a bowtied suit. A handsome and well-preserved older gentleman. He talks in a tone and authority that eases you, convinces you and lulls you. And that is the point.

His job kit is comprised of merely a briefcase full of lead weights and, you guessed it, a broom. That's it. The hustle that isn't even a hustle, it's just a fair contest of strength. He often runs this challenge on privileged, steroid enthusiast fraternity boys, and when he does, it's beautiful. I have never seen anyone top it before or since. I feel like he's in Santa Barbara half the year and New Orleans the other half. I don't think he told me that it's just a vibe I get. Each fall and winter, he brings back a light Robert Johnsonesque Voodoo essence to the scene. He sure can smoke a joint down to the fingertips quick too.

There is a small plaza between the parking lot and the sidewalk that leads past the reggae spot, Calypso, down on to Toe's Tavern. It's dollar beer night at Toe's so the foot traffic is thick. The jocks are primed to get 'Fucked up!' and harass some chicks. To get to Toe's, they have to pass my friend and pot customer, Clarence, the Broom Man, who is knowingly waiting for them. "Hey there, young men. Can I show you something right quick?"

The puffed-out frat boys stop to see what this presumptuous black man might have to say to them. I mean, does he not know his place or what? They turn their swollen, spread out arms to face him on their bow legs. "Yeah. What's up, bud?"

Clarence is sizing them up to see how much to try and get them for at first. A fiver? No...$20. "You look like strong, powerful young men. How would you like to make a wager in a test of strength between yourselves and yours truly?"

"Ha ha. Are you kidding me, old man? Ha ha. You're old, dude," says the guy with an upside-down and backward visor and a ZBT fraternity shirt.

This gives the other meathead with the spaghetti strap tank top the confidence to levy a fifth-grade level roast himself. "Wow! Is this, like, going to be a trick or something? Don't scam us, bro. You weigh like a buck sixty. I was benching like two of you an hour ago," he says, puffing out his chest when he gets to the word 'benching.'

Clarence unfurls his shtick with his usual sing-songy flair. "It's no trick, no illusion. All you must do is lift the broom with a small lead weight on the bristled end. Easy as pie for strapping young lads such as yourselves. Shall we say $20? What you see before you *is* indeed a man of some years and of slight stature, but I assure you that I was born with an unusually strong hand. I am telling you now that I will be able to do it. But can you?

That's all you have to do. A tie goes to you. Now, I will show you that I can do it."

Clarence grabs the end of the broom's handle and lifts the weighted end in a perfectly flat, horizontal fashion, with more agility than he should be able to muster for a man of 60. The 10-pound lead weight is over a yard out in front. He lowers it down to the ground, but not in a hurry. At this point, without even having made a bet, Clarence has these chumps in his pocket. A small crowd has gathered, and there is no way these musclebound idiots are going to leave without lifting that broom in the air. It's Clarence's broom, so they **will** have to pay to play. There are witnesses now—more gathering up every second. The frat boys are stuck.

"Ok, ok, that's easy," one of them says.

Tweedle-Dee is reaching for his wallet, but it's hard to reach that part of his protein engorged body. He gets it finally, hangs the bill in the air, then pulls it back a little, prompting Clarence to prove that he has the money to cover the bet. A bill with a genocidal white man on the front of it is rapidly produced from a decent sized roll, and both $20s are placed, fanned out between the weight and the broom bristles. The jock grabs the end of the broom handle from the ground and begins the attempted lift. "Hhhrrrrrrnnnnnn, gaaaaaahhhhhh!"

The weighted end doesn't budge off the ground. Tweedle-Dee lowers the handle 3-inches until his knuckles are almost touching the sidewalk, and he tries again. "Aaaaaaarnahhhhh!" This time he drops the handle. He's beaten.

If you don't believe it, try it at home, folks. Put a dozen eggs on some broom bristles, and see if you can lift it. The physics of lifting a weight that is *that* far out in front of you is hard to understand, but that doesn't make it less real.

The other meathead grabs his own $20 bill and offers it up to the challenge just to suffer the same fate. They waddle away in shame as the crowd looks at Clarence with adoration and wonder. Clarence looks at me and says, "You holdin'? Dey all in the bahs now. Let 'em git drunk, an' I'll catch 'em on da way out. Time for a fortitude adjustment. Know what I mean, Jellybean?"

"Yeah, I got some weed." We walk off to a decent smoke spot where we can get high. He drops the Queen's English act, angling for a good deal on some dirt weed in his preferred dialect.

"Come own, mayng! Dis chit dahrtier den a bottle a Keet Richardss peeeiss, muh-fuckah. I guess I'll let you git about half a dat las' win, you drop one mo bud'n deyah. You take one 'o dem boys twenties and pack me up wid a bag big enough to take me aaaaallll da way ta sleep."

"All right, Clarence, that sounds good to me."

It's always good hanging with Clarence. Cool dude. I always give him an extra bud in "deyah." He's my hero. He is just punishing egos wherever he goes without having to risk a bloody nose to do it like me, a true champion. I always tried to figure out how he does it, suspecting it's a trick at first, but there's no fishing line, he doesn't hitch it on the underside of his forearm. Nothin'.

I watch him a hundred times from every angle. There's nothing but his bare hand and the very end of the broom handle. None of the handle's end goes into the sleeve or anything. I pay a few times to try it myself.

I almost sprain my wrist and don't feel like I'm even lifting half. At $5 a shot, I don't need to try on more than two occasions. It's like an Arthurian, back-alley, sword and stone challenge.

So, I get to know him, and I realize when I shake his large hand, it's like putting your hand inside a railroad safe. He has a bunch of ten-pound lead weights in his briefcase. He carries it all day long in his right hand, twisting and working his wrist and forearm. One time, smoking with him on a hot day, he takes off his suit jacket, giving a rare view of the kind of shape this 'mystery arm' is in. The shoulder and bicep *are* bigger on the right side, but when you get to the forearm and wrist? It's like a different body! Talk about Popeye the Sailor Man.

This skinny old man has been blasting machismo through absolutely no trick or treachery, except for keeping everything lean except where it counts. I suppose he doesn't exactly show off that grapefruit forearm either; wearing a suit jacket even in summer, but still never sweating. He's beating pseudo-manliness at its own game. Rigorous weight training and some sort of genetic ability to lock his wrist? It's not steroids; the rest of his body wouldn't have stayed that skinny. The guy is too classy for that garbage anyway. Amazing. Here's to you, Clarence, The Broom Man. If I see you around, I always have a big ass joint with your name on it, you mildly Rasta-Cajun sounding assed, bluesman on his daughter's wedding day looking, magical motherfucker.

Got to Get Out

Moving downtown wasn't enough to get a fresh start in life. I mean, the guy who ratted me out for weed was a customer I'd dragged with me from Isla Vista, just eight miles down the road. It's like I switched from whiskey to vodka. A nice gesture, with a bit of practicality, but hardly the distance one needs to go to straighten this shit out.

I hear Shipley's family has started a restaurant in Hawaii. Immediately, I decide that I will bartend there. It's on the other side of the world, and that sounds almost far enough to leave this place behind—this place which drags me over the broken glass of hometown stagnation every night.

It's just mai tais and piña coladas over there, right? I'll drink a controllable amount of booze—on the house, of course—and make the ladies laugh. What is the word? Serendipity. It feels like the timing of this is destiny. Forget the fact that Shipley is from there and probably has a lot of lifelong friends and family in line for the gravy jobs. Why would I need a resume? Shipley's a homie.

My head is in dreamland as I call and subtly insinuate that I'll bring over a bunch of green buds. To this, Shipley instantly agrees and even says they could probably set me up with a job. After all, an ounce of green bud is worth almost a thousand bucks on Oahu. As rare as an orchid on mars. Seed money. Check.

I scrounge, save, and call in a few favors until I finally come up with enough for a one-way plane ticket to Hawaii and an ounce of green bud from Motormouth Scotty. I tape up the sticky bud in bags made from NASA developed plastic that is so nonporous it hides the smell of even the most ultra-permeable pot. *Even* from police dogs and that dude at the party who always seems to know who is holding.

I tape the bag down into a highly compact, baseball-sized nugget, shove it into my butt hugger underwear, nervously walk into LAX, and get on a plane to Honolulu.

On the plane, I try to figure out how I got to this crossroads where I'm fleeing to the most remote island chain in the ocean with $50 in my pocket and a felony in my ball sack. Is it the sadness of my mom's lack of planning, the resulting homelessness, and the general lack of resources that plagued my teen years? Yes, partly, but I've processed that. There must be more to it than that.

I spent a few high school years and all my summers at Dad's. What damage was inflicted on my psyche from *that* experience? A lot, I think. I try to remember the best times with him, and it turns out even *those* were full of machismo and the toxicity of having to be number one.

As I sit on the plane, I drift off into a fond memory of being with my Dad. I try to analyze it pragmatically for my mental wellbeing.

I daydream back ten or a dozen years ago: *"You got that ski on yet, boy?!"* *My dad barks from the captain's chair on the boat*~~

I fumble with the binding and the life jacket straps, which are too loose and pinning my upper lip to my teeth. I'm shivering because I'm skinny as a goal post, and it's a cold, early desert morning at Lake Mohave. You have to go at the butt crack of dawn because that's when the water is smoothest. "Br-a-lmost, Dad."

"I see a boat pullin' a kid just a little bigger kid than you! Get that ski on, and we'll get up alongside 'em!! You jump that whole wake and moon him in his face!! Come on, boy!!"

These are the good times. Everybody eases up and relaxes a little bit. Not too much, of course, a Scales keeps composure; a rigid attack mode must be vigilantly pursued at all moments, even in your sleep! Other families would surely be looking for the title of *Most Awesome Motherfuckers on the Lake!*

We might not have the fastest speed boats, but we can *and will* outrun any other boats that are pulling kids on skis. It's the kid's limits that are tested then, not the boats. My Dad will instantly sense where another ship is dragging a kid that's just a little bigger than my sisters or me, depending on where we're at in the rotation. Many a preteen boy has had to walk head down on the beach for having just been smoked in the two-mile dash by one of my sisters on a knee-ski. I remember they made one kid shave off his only pubic hair. They said he didn't deserve it.

One such afternoon, we're navigating through a narrow spot with high cliffs on both sides. Our boat's engine is gurgling as we slow down to a drift. *Glllllllrrrgllle, ggllllllrrrgggllleee, braaaattttttttt, blllllllaaaaaaarrrrrraaaaattttttt!!!!!*

Just then, on the starboard side, a teenager drops from 50-feet above and smacks hard into the water.

What *you* see is a kid jumping off a cliff and having fun, but what it *really* is? Coliseum training. That kid howls with the trademark hoot of his family before casting himself off the high crags of potential death. If your hoot or howl cracks as you jump, it's over. No fear can echo through the canyon. If you send a shockwave of terror if you *do* plummet from a cackle of insanity into a shriek of a scared Japanese schoolgirl? It just multiplies itself and echoes back, again and again, high over the fractal rings of boats, rafts, and tubes full of critics and judges. Judges, who themselves have trouble stepping off a high curb—much less tossing yourself off of a jagged cliff. This irony seems to be unappreciated by these jeering critics who only stare and expect.

The kid finally comes back up. A ripple of fearful sighs and gasps answer from the boats, which are full of the mothers and the sisters of the death challenging teenage boys. He panicked his way into a belly flop. Mom is crying.

For the next jumper, it will be a better day than that. This particular family howl is well executed and immediately followed by a leap, a delayed knee tuck, and last-second centrifugal flip *sliishhhh!* Nothing at the slightly broken plane to suggest such a massive arc of power just ended there. A perfect entry! It's as if his body straightens out at the last possible moment and unzips the water with his toes. He slides in like it's a familiar sleeping bag. And what a, *"Whay-ay-ay-oooooot!"* he started it with.

It's still echoing when the crowd loses it, a family howl, which appears to have traces in its more recent history in Appalachia and its less recent from Scotland. A cross between a *Braveheart* death growl and a *Deliverance*-y threat overture. And he's like 12yo! Competition is stiff today.

Points are subconsciously given, groupthink style, and subtracted for the overall base level of the howl. This one is a winner. I imagine what the names for all the forms of jumping are, backflip toe tucks? Wobble-Flops? Quadruple-dapple-Gainers? Jesus-pose ass-Slapper? Which jump will I be expected to attempt? It's essential to choose the right jump in the *hierarchal establishment of family ratings* on the lake regarding pure *ball having-ness*. **That** is the championship belt that outshines all others at the lake—Best BBQers is a tumorish comparison—Biggest Brass Balls is the **only** belt a Scales can accept. It's the one my Dad used to get us, and now it's on me, the skinny artistic kid who's half my, 'welfare collecting mother,' and enjoys reading. Great. The only thing a Scales should ever "enjoy reading" is the obituaries of his crushed enemies. To this side of my family, my dogeared copy of Grapes of Wrath is seen as a sort of disability. If not for my trademark Scales forehead, I would have been dropped off at the milkman's house long ago in flat denial of my supposed DNA.

We eventually get to the spot way back in the cove. The place Dad had probably jumped into manhood about 27 years ago. Now it will be me. I don't know it as we begin into the canyon, but I will soon. At least I'm a natural jumper. I sprained my ankle at two. I was attempting to break the record for the *baby long jump* off the dinner table. I perfected doing flips off the apartment building roof into Bird of Paradise bushes years ago.

We pass the baby jump that the preteens are jumping off, which is maybe 15-feet. Across the canyon to our right, there is an 80-foot jump that a couple of psychotic guys are leaping from. The biggest crowd of the day is up there at the midsize cliff. That's where the 15 and up crowd is jumping from. I roll my eyes as we pass by the baby jump. I have to practically throw gang signs at the little cowards who are jumping off it. *East Side Vikings, bitch! I got my first pubic hair!*

If I show any weakness, my pit-bull sisters will be tapped in; my 11yo sister will end up being snookered into attempting a Double-barrel-anchor-Bomb. It's madness, but the ship is at sea. The laws of land don't bind a man at sea. Vikings don't have the longest or even the funnest lives, but they are truly free out on the open water. Presently, I am about to earn my Viking horns or swim back to Riverside.

My father gets us just outside the impact zone and looks back at me with only three words. Three words which speak library shelves, "All right, boy."

I am out of the boat quick because I know there is no avoiding it. If I can prove to have more heart than it looks like my skinny legs can carry, then I can get back on the boat. Soon, I'm swimming toward the vertical face.

I am a Scales. I can and *will* outdo any kid who threatens my family's testicular superiority, newly functional as it is. My sisters bark out to me like dire wolves, "Do a flip! Do a Leg-poker-Backflip!"

It's late afternoon, the sun has turned the mountain range orangey-red. The top of the mountain range in one direction looks like an Indian chief laying on his back as if on a funeral pyre, complete with headdress. If you are ever at Lake Mohave, look for that, you'll see it if you have any kind of imagination.

I pull myself up out of the water at the base of the immense vertical cliff. A wind blows up off the water and into my shorts, freezing my apricots even smaller. Biggest balls on the lake. What a joke.

I start working my way up this giant thing, and it just seems to stretch further on up with each tiny gain I make with my skinny, shaky legs. What am I, insane? Why do I have to be the proof? Just because I'm the only male Scales in my generation? Because the name will end with me if I don't procreate? The weight of this jump has hinged on it the very **future** of the Scales empire. The expectant stares of my clan radiate this fact through my soul as I climb upward towards Sparta and Alpha-dom.

In the boats below, I imagine them whispering about the last kid who climbed the 60-foot cliff that was my age. Just two hours ago, he Wobble-Flopped and capitulated into a haphazard side-splatter and passed out face down in the water. His family just left him there to drift into some reeds while they packed up their beach tent and went back home to Corona.

Now, I have to do it. I make a mistake and look down, and instantly my depth perception goes on the fritz, and I get dizzy. *Look up, or they'll see the fear in your face, stupid.* The bottom is so far down my eyes can't even perceive it. Fuck this. These people are going to get me killed. I freak out, and in a fleeting moment of weakness, I blindly probe back down a step with my timid chicken leg. I can't just jump down from halfway because of the hump that has to be cleared.

"This is America. Do you know who doesn't have humps jutting out at you as you fall into adulthood? Those fuckin' Russians," I imagine the fathers muttering below. They remember themselves when they were young and perfect, and they superimpose their faces onto ours as we jump. *This time we won't Wobble-Flop,* they think, as they gamble with our futures.

People come partly to see if something terrible happens. That's part of the allure. The possibility of a free adrenaline high when you see a kid bounce off a rock and belly flop into a lake from higher than a tipped up semi-trailer.

Now I'm up here, and it seems like everybody is making this the headline event. I am too young to be doing this jump. The light is fading quickly.

The kids from the kiddie jump have floated back to the motherships and swell the crowd even bigger. They get here just in time to see me either shame them or kill myself, bringing in a hater element that I feel helps me. These new spectators, they want my blood. If I succeed, they will have to return tomorrow and do the jump themselves or just admit defeat and ski in pink shorts. I feel their hatred pierce into me as I perplexedly gauge the hump, the landing, and my potential for a maximum spring out. I breathe in until I am lightheaded.

Ok, you can do it, J.C. Don't freak out and piss your OP cords, dude. Nothing fancy, just survive the jump and don't flop, flip or side slap. Just land as straight as Tom Cruise pretends to be. Breathe out. Breathe in. You are a genius...you are a beast... you have been tapped for greatness. You have a duty, and a gift to be outrageous and magnificent—way up ahead of where anybody could expect you to be. Something magic is in you!

I jump while I can still believe these high estimations. The dead Indian chief laying on his back blurs, and I am already halfway down, and the adrenaline hits me for real. I forget my family howl, but finally, just before impact, *"Haaayyyyyhayhaaaayyyyyyttttttt!!!!!! Chhhaaaaaaaaaa!!!!!"*

It's a sort of naked, mud-coated berserker, storming a beach, high on lotus, kind of thing—very attention-getting, very black plague-ish. My voice doesn't crack, and I get it all out, barely. The wind fills my shorts, and I feel myself go a tiny bit crooked. Shit. I land pretty straight but kind of smash my shoulder coming in and feel my body create what was probably a huge imbalanced splash. I'm alive, but sinking deeper, out of air already because of my late howl. Also, my elbow slapping into my ribs took the little wind I had left at impact.

I fight my way to the top with a panicky gasp inward at the surface. I suck in a little water and choke a little bit, which isn't elegant, but nobody cares. They can't believe I did it!

Once I get a breath, my ears explode from the insane crowd! Even the 13yo kids that I just ruined the grade curve for look impressed. The whole canyon is booming and shouting. People are all shouting different things, but one thing is clear, they are all looking at me with eyes that perceive greatness! Oh, the look on my grandma's face! The relief on my sisters' faces that they won't have to be called to save the family honor. We are the *King Shits of the Lake!*

It's true; nobody jumped after that. I jump last and best that day. It's the first time I ever just absolutely slay on one of the world's big stages! Quite intoxicating. I'm hooked! **Convincing people to attempt more than they're supposed to attempt in life**—will be the mission statement of my empire built on courage. I know now what the cornerstones of my benevolent foundation will be: **"Balls! Pure balls!"**

Bathing in that vanity, I temporarily lose myself. I know now that being a Scales is all it's cracked up to be. I used to deny it because I was preparing myself to deal with the possible disappointment of not being allowed to even *be* a Scales. Now I know. The Viking life is short, but oh so sweet!

My Grandpa talks to me more that night, even though he's the strong silent type. I think it was the first time I'd made him proud. It felt amazing to bask in his love.

After our BBQ at the beach campfire that night, we are all making victory S' mores. We imagine all the jealous fuckers looking down to our part of the beach, wondering how much they would have to shine our shoes tomorrow. My sisters haven't even pulled out their knee-skis yet. Would we be coming for their preteens with my sisters tomorrow? We would. Surely, we would.

Perhaps one of my sisters would be the champion tomorrow, but for now, I'm the favored hero of the family. Anybody can be the hero on any given day, that's a fact about the Viking life—but today it's me!

Returning from my dazed and deep recollection of that fantastic family river trip, I consider the implications of all this. It appears that *yes*, my Dad has fucked me up just as much as my mom has. NASCAR's America has tainted me. I am an adrenaline freak. Permanently—and a macho man.

Getting *Lei*'d

Recovered now from my daydreaming, the pilot announces our final descent into Honolulu. There is a growing discomfort in my nutsack region. I start shifting and scrunching because this jagged tape ball full of weed is just grinding into my balls as the moist jungle developing inside my jeans gets itchy and desperate. The guy next to me seems like he thinks I have crabs, and the middle armrest is all mine for the last little strand of the flight.

We get off the plane, and there is a row of hula girls putting the traditional flower necklaces called *Leis* around everyone's neck. Nice touch.

I see one police dog by the luggage carousels, and I have a small panic attack followed by a river of sweat down my face. I've got to get this ball torturing bag of weed out of my pants before I have to strip down and hysterically streak my way out of here. That would be sad too because my balls and dick are trying to run up inside of my belly like a paranoid hermit crab right now. My junk is so deep up in there I'm afraid if I pissed myself in fear, it would stream out my asshole. That would not be the greatest first impression to the island I plan on making my home for a while.

Please, Dave, be out front. Where are you? I am safely out into the pick-up area, a pleasing development, and I'm craning my neck around desperately as Dave pulls up with his girlfriend in a convertible. *Nice!* I hop in, and as soon as we're out of the pick-up area, I reach down and pull out the apple of doom from my pants and kick it under the front seat. "Ahhhh! How are you guys? I feel so much better now. Thank you for picking me up. That flight seemed like...forever."

Dave turns his ponytailed head in his seat and gives me a concerned look. "Welcome to Hawaii. We're going to get you real comfortable. You bring presents?"

"Yeah, Dave, don't worry. The restaurant is opening this week, right? I need a job, man. I want to stay here. I'll get a place soon, ok?" All my thoughts come spilling out of my mouth, full of nervous excitement, worry, and hope.

"Yeah, don't worry. In Hawaii, it all works out. You want to work? We got you, but the restaurant is taking a bit longer than we thought to open."

Dave's volume drops a bit on that last part. Who cares? It's beautiful here, the smell of the *Lei* that the hula girls put on me is intoxicating, along with the salty wind coming off of Waikiki. Shit, I'll sleep on the beach if I have to. Didn't Dave just say, "In Hawaii, it all works out"?

We wind up into a neighborhood to the top of a hill. There is a trailhead on the side of the house that goes back into the old lava flow. The porch overlooks the south shore of Oahu, right down into Diamond Head.

After that, it's just an endless blue sea between me and my former problems. Amazing. I feel delivered.

The family is welcoming. I sleep in the same room as Dave's mom, with just a partition between us. This saint of a woman tolerated my snores for weeks. Crazy that a family would be this welcoming to someone who is clearly fleeing a crap situation without much of a plan. Their complete lack of judgment or boundary setting is very therapeutic for me. I feel better as I drink light beers on their porch, drawing art for the restaurant, doing push-ups, getting my mind sharp, letting the cocaine filter out of my body.

I skateboard from the house down the hill through the University of Oahu into Waikiki and swim in the warm waters in front of the Hilton's Happy Hawaiian Village. In the evenings when Dave gets home, we smoke my ever-dwindling sack of killer green bud, laugh, and talk about how great the restaurant is going to be.

One day, I go to the restaurant and paint the bathrooms. They seem like they are still *a ways out* from the big opening. Things in Hawaii move slow. No one is in a hurry to do anything, which is relaxing but can also be a double-edged sword. Some evenings, we go out to the bars. "Hey, Samson? This is my buddy, J.C. Take care of him. Don't let him get into trouble, ok? Wild one, dis guy, don't let da face fool you," Dave says to a giant Samoan security guard one evening.

"Oh, you buddies wit' Dave? Anyting you want, bruddah! Just let me know," says Samson, as he turns to me with a big smile and bright eyes. Samson shakes my hand vigorously, almost shaking it off to clink and clank down into his massive paw. "Oh, ok. Um, I'm good for now, Samson. Thanks, man!"

You might be thinking this is a different experience that a Haole boy from the Mainland might expect to have with a Samoan on Oahu. I'd have to say that you are correct in thinking that. But Dave and his father are the top surf judges in Hawaii, which essentially makes them the presidents of the entire island chain. Fuckin' Dave's Dad founded a major surf company. Holy shit!

I was vaguely aware of that in Santa Barbara, but back then, Dave just seemed like a regular surfer dude. Always smiling and smoking weed. Here, he's a celebrity.

I probably could have told Samson to "Drop and give me 20," and he would have done it, but I don't want to push my luck. Instead, I smile at him and rescue my hand before making my way to the bar. It's nice to know I can talk trash in here and have the support of a *violence mountain*. That's the type of shit that usually comes in handy to me, as I am often loudly correcting people's behavior at parties and bars. It's my way of being a vigilante. It doesn't always go smoothly.

One night, we go to Saigon Nights strip club with Marky; think corn-fed Jeff Spicolli, and Jay Woo; toothy Tasmanian devil who only smiles if you say something funny *or* if he's decided at which 'big guy' at the party he's going to yell, "Hey you! Big fuck! Why you give me stink eye, bruddah?! Gonna be hawd to leef doze weights wid a fawkin' brohhken leg, bruddah!!"

Like Shipley, Jay Woo is from here. Great guys, Marky and Jay Woo. They're like the Irish and Australians. Great fun, but you gotta ditch them before midnight. Otherwise, it's just swan diving Gremlins everywhere. You got the fuckin' Gremlins wet, bro—by that, I mean you bought Marky has magic number 6th shot of tequila.

Marky has been living here a year and wants to be Hawaiian so bad he's insisting on speaking Hawaiian slang—*pigeon*. He's not terrible at it, but you can still tell he's just a rich kid from La Jolla. He's a big dude, so he can get away with it, I guess. All I know is if *I* tried talking to some big moke in his own dialect, I'd get the shit slapped out of me. I might need to get a, "I know Shipley," laminated badge if these guys are getting all crazy in Waikiki.

I know these guys from when they were enrolled in college in Santa Barbara. I was with Mark one of my first times freebasing. We smoked the baking soda fried cocaine out of a broken car antenna. This was around the time me, him, and Jay tried to fight the entire Toe's Tavern security team. That ended with me getting cartwheeled through a palm bush onto State Street and Jay breaking a few fingers on one of them from the bottom of a pile. All because they wouldn't let Marky's drunk ass back in the bar to get his credit card. Anyway, it was instant friends with me, Mark, and Jay. It's good to see them again. Classic dudes.

We all watch the girls as they dance seductively on the pole in an attempt to get dollars out of our pockets. Dollars that—for most of us present—don't exist. "We're here for you ladies, don't feel unloved, but our wallets are here strictly for the $3 happy hour beers."

It's nice to be able to laugh at the alcoholic escapades of last year through rose-colored binoculars, safely in the middle of the Pacific. The nights are warm, you can smell flowers on the breeze, and the cheap beer goes down smooth. All is well.

The next day we go surfing at a place called Suicides. The 40yo longboard I've been loaned as a joke gets away from me, and I have to chase it a quarter-mile across a shallow reef. Waves toss me among the jagged rock, razor-sharp barnacles, mussels, and the healthy crops of spiny urchins, who invite me to hell. The guys thought it was pretty funny. Ha-ha, fuckers.

And that's how a few weeks roll by. I'm pretty much having a blast until the pot is all smoked. Meanwhile, the *grand opening* of Shipley's Ale House and Grill is still having delays. Another month on rent will have to be paid for it before they can open the doors. Ouch.

Kel's Couch Again

After a few weeks, my weed supply is almost gone, and Shipley hasn't sold any $100 bags so I can rent another place somewhere. Also, the only job they can offer me is food prepping in the kitchen for $8 an hour. This, in a town where rent is $800 a month. *Fuck.* "My mom wants to know what your plans are," says Shipley. International code for *You have two days to bounce.*

"Well shit, I tried to plan it, so I got here on the grand opening. Now all my weed is gone. I'll call Kel on Maui." I call her, she picks up, and I let out a held breath. "Hey."

"What's up, J.C.? So good to hear from you. You sound close."

"I am," I say.

"Well, are you comin' over?"

"Could I?"

"Of course! When?"

"Tomorrow?" I hang out on a thin branch.

"Um, well, I have something going on tomorrow."

"That's cool. I'm sorry to always appear on your doorstep on short notice. It's ok if you're busy," I say, defeat audible in my voice.

"No. I want you to come. Come in three days," says Kel, the constant lifesaver of me.

I am ecstatic, and my excitement probably betrays my desperation.

"Ok, thanks, Kel! It's going to be fun! Just like the old days."

The old days were only seven years ago, but when you're not even 25, it qualifies.

Kel gets serious for a minute while trying to sound casual, "When is your return ticket?"

Hesitation, followed up by, "Well…I thought I'd leave it open-ended."

"Shit, J.C." The cat has scratched its way out of the bag again. Oopsie.

"You still want me to come?" I regret saying as soon as it comes out.

What if she says, "No"? I would have to fucking swim back to California. I tapped all my resources to get here, and I am **not** going back to Santa Barbara with my tail between my legs. Fuck that. I would rather be a homeless beach bum here. The second before she speaks seems to take an eternity.

"No, come. Come." Music to my ears.

Three days later, I am on an island hopper to Kihei, Maui, where I catch a bus into Lahaina and find Kel. She's living in a place off Front Street at the edge of the main strip, whose beginning is marked with a humungous banyan tree that takes up a city block, roots falling from the branches, and rejoining the earth, creating the look of a forest made of one tree. This is a spot that the neighborhood seeks out on the hotter days. King Kamehameha had his parties here back in the day as this was the capital of Hawaii before the whites showed up and fucked it all up. For about five blocks after *The Banyan* there are non-stop bars, restaurants, souvenir shops, and art galleries featuring whale paintings that cost as much as a factory-fresh Porsche.

Kel knows everyone in town because she is one of the greatest all-star charmers in history. She has a perfect white-toothed smile that beams at you from the upside-down triangle that is her beautiful cheekbones and endlessly cute chin. Curly auburn hair cascades down her confident shoulders. Meet her for a minute, and you would do just about anything she says. I have seen her convince the neighbors that the band 'won't be that loud,' and, 'could we run the amp plugins through your back window?' I have watched her save, moderate, and instigate more parties than Mötley Crüe's band manager.

She was one of our best soldiers back in Isla Vista. Her secret weapon is that you would never suspect that face of doing anything other than giving you a painful crush. By the time you realize that she is *Shiva, Destroyer of House Parties*, it's too late, your booze is gone, and your coffee table has been reduced to splinters.

I find her in Lahaina continuing the war against boredom with her typical flamboyant panache. A slightly tamer, more tropical version. She instantly gets me a job. Not a great one, but I have no resume, and up until a month ago, I was a ragged coke head with dirty underwear and a lousy attitude. The new me hasn't had a chance to define itself yet. So, it looks like I am going to be working the door at Cheeseburgers in Paradise. I'm the hostess! I'm so broke. I have to buy used white shoes from the thrift store, and they are a size too small. I go sockless to make them fit better, and by the first week, the heat has fermented my foot stink into the previous wearer's until they morph into a nostril sensation that would make the Egyptian Sphinx cut off its nose again.

The friendly gay managers are kind enough to supply me with some white shorts that are even tighter than the shitty shoes I bought. This uniform from hell gives me more reasons to squirm back and forth as I greet the customers with a, "Welcome to Cheeseburgers in Paradise, would you like a table by the window?"

The managers are cruising by every five minutes to study any asymmetry in my camel toe and to tell me, "Your smile is your biggest asset. *Smiiiiile.*" All this as my balls and toes throb telegraphic pain to each other.

After a month of this shit, I'm ready to throw a customer in the fuckin' ocean. Any table you try to give 'em, they think you're trying to trick them into taking the table with the trap door or something. "Oh, this table? Yeah, maybe not. Hmmm. Well, those people are almost done," gesturing to the largest table we have, currently occupied by six people who just barely got their appetizers. That's the table they think *they* are getting, even though they only have three in their party.

"Maybe we'll have a drink at the bar and wait for *that* table," the Rubenesque Idahoan ladies instruct, as they walk away, signaling that this wasn't to be a negotiation. Their Carnival Cruise isn't going to be trifled with by a lowly restaurant greeter with visibly lopsided junk trying to twist its way out of the bottom of some short shorts. Every 20 minutes, the Jimmy Buffet song that the restaurant is themed after comes on, "*Cheeseburgers in Paradise!*" I want to kill everyone I see, but instead, I have to force a twisted smile.

Paying your dues as a broke white kid from the Mainland is not fantastic. 'Fuckin' Haoles,' the natives, call us, as they watch us eat plates of shit for tiny amounts of money. If they catch us trying to surf, talking to any local girls, or separated from our friends, they give us a good beat down and tell us, "Go back to da Mainland, Haole **fawk** head!" *Slap!*

In addition to that, the pay at work is as garbage as the work itself. I supplement my income by schooling the people that live in Kel's building at poker. After everyone gets done with their restaurant jobs, it's cheaper just to get a few fifths of rum and play cards than going to the bars. I'm winning about $300 per week, and everyone gets so shitfaced that they wake up not remembering if they won or lost, looking in their pockets at their tips and going, "I guess I didn't make as much last night as I thought."

I see them in the mornings as everyone scratches their groggy heads, and I say, "Damn, who won last night? I got ravaged."

"Not me," they say.

One night, me and Kelly are sitting on her couch, and she says, "People think you're my boyfriend. Isn't that funny?"

"Ha-ha. Yeah, that's hilarious." I say.

Did she just toss her hair back when she said that? J.C.? I know the islands have been very dry for you—It's true. Something about mega-poverty in unfamiliar territories throws my game off—but do not try to fuck your friend. Not even your friend, that's basically your sister.

Ok, ok. Shit dude. Stop breaking my balls. I thought she threw her hair back.

After what must have seemed like forever, Kel's very tolerant and cool roommates, Carrie and Dave, have her get rid of me. A Cito Rat named Razor needs a roommate—one of the rich derelict kids from the Montecito side of Santa Barbara, where Oprah lives. Richest of the rich and big problems to match their parent's bank accounts—some guy named Razor. The rent is $700. A fair deal for a famous tourist town like Lahaina. The timeshare victims are paying more than that just for a weekend. I accept that I will have to start paying rent, and I move into the cinderblock house with linoleum peeling up from the floor.

Some advice? Never move into a house with a guy named Razor. As I shave and get ready for my degrading job in the mornings, Razor comes in the bathroom and tells me how suicidal he is. He's a heroin addict. He sucks. His negativity is palpable in the next room. He just babbles on about how much his life sucks. He has a girlfriend who puts up with this, and she's pretty. I can't figure it out. Fuckin' rich kids, man. They are more fucked up than us gutter urchins, that's for sure.

Better to grow up in the middle. In America, we have somewhat of a middle class in 1996. That's the trick, being middle class. All I want is enough money so that I don't have to worry, but not so much that *all* I do is worry. I'm not asking for too much in life, and I'm willing to bust my ass to be middle class. Someone just give me a fuckin' chance. Getting me out of this shithole house living with Razor would be a good start.

I'm getting depressed living with this guy. There are heroin needles in the bathroom trash all the time. The first time I open the fridge to put in some hard-earned groceries, I see that it hasn't been in working order for quite some time. The temperature is the same as the top of the roof, and there has been enough time for a long-forgotten block of cheese to fill an entire corner with a neon green mold. The nasty fur seems to pulsate and shimmer. So, this is where Razor keeps his decrepit spirit. It looks like I'm sponsoring a BBQ at Kel's.

I simply have got to find new digs. Maybe if I get Banks to move over here, we can use any credit rating he might have and split the cost of a one-bedroom lease.

Logistical Oversight

Banks is coming! I convinced him I'm doing great over here, and that I have a job for him, which isn't entirely true. In reality, I am having trouble keeping my *own* job. After three months in this town, I have as much pull as a megachurch preacher at a Slayer concert. But I need a wingman, so I have to lie to him. Everything turns out fine. I knew it would, and sometimes that's all that matters. Well, at least it turns out fine for Banks. As for how things turn out for me, that's all up to perspective.

First, we celebrate. Banks arrives, and we all go on a whale watch, because Kel knows somebody on the boat, of course. Free appetizers and mai tais with cheap rum. Shortly after landing, we end up at Hecock's Bar.

"Banks, look at those beautiful balconies. You could climb up the front of them and jump in the pool," I say to Banks, as we look out the open window at the Lahaina Shores Hotel.

"J.C.?" begins Banks in a highly concerned tone. "Don't do it! Look! Half the pool is under the awning. You'll have to drop straight down so close to the building the magnetic pull will slam you back into it! You ever drop a grape off a high balcony? It turns into juice halfway down."

"Oh, yeah?" I say, recalling my favorite childhood phrase.

I finish my syrupy cocktail with the little white and purple orchid garnish and hop out through the window of the bar, over a bird of paradise bush, up the wooden railed balcony of Lahaina Shores Hotel, and up to about the seventh floor.

I have about a four-foot target, as half the pool is underneath the building, just like Banks said. Plenty of room, I figure. So, I hang my spine vertical along with my outward-facing limbs two-feet directly out from the side of the building. Over the middle of the part of the pool that isn't under the building. The other two limbs are hinged onto the balcony, trying to afford the perfect balance before I instantaneously twitch out and down.

I am drunk, but not that drunk. I sort of know what I'm doing. I don't encourage you to look at this as a bright thing to do. It isn't, and I pay the piper, but I don't die.

So, there I go from the seventh floor. From there, my target seems like a little blue lit up strip. Like a microfilm picture of the ocean looked at against the window. As I'm sailing down towards the eight-foot-deep pool, I realize the pool is eight-feet deep, but I don't have eight-feet of water because I'm six-feet tall. Technically, two-feet is what I seem to have. Well, this is quite the pickle to discover halfway down. At the very least, a medium-sized logistical oversight.

Five stories...four...three...ok, what I'm going to do is after my ankles go under the water, I'll go into cannonball position and take a big shot to the ass, upper legs, and the bottom of my arms.

That's what I do, and my work shorts rip from the perineum to the small of my back. I fart out a half pint of water from a bruised colon. I miss a day of work from the bruises that stretch from the back of my knees to my asshole, forearms, and even my palms. I live, bruised and a bit raped, but Banks said I couldn't do it. And that's how he arrives in Maui. This is gonna be sweet.

Ali'i

I get shit-canned from Cheeseburgers in Paradise for telling an unusually bitch-ass customer to go fuck himself, and my tone wasn't very polite, "allegedly." Soon, I am working for this apartment manager painting units. Ali'i is his name. I meet him when he picks me up hitchhiking from Ka'anapali, the next town up the road where I like to swim sometimes to get away from the hyper-touristic area that is Lahaina. It's a gorgeous beach with a rock jump into the ocean. There's reasonably priced beer at a little joint by the water. Perfect escape.

Ali'i is a 60yo Hawaiian dude with a bunch of gold rings and necklaces, an unbuttoned silk Hawaiian shirt, and rounding out the look is a werewolf's amount of black and grey chest hair. Wait, I almost forgot the impressive Elvis-style pompadour. I take this all in spontaneously as I jump into the worn leather passenger seat. An experienced hitchhiker learns to look for problems, even as he or she is hurriedly hopping into a vehicle that may or may not still be rolling. In an instant, one must assess potential dangers. He or she must ask themselves questions such as *Is this guy smiling too big? Is there nothing but rope and a jar of Crisco in the backseat? Are there 'Jesus on cassette' tapes strewn about? The front plates—did they say Florida?* If any of these dangers are perceived, it may be time to open the door and roll out sideways. I don't perceive any issues and give a standard polite greeting, "Hey man, thanks."

He responds with, "Where you headed, bruddah?"

"Lahaina," I say.

"Cool, dat's wayah I'm a headed too. You woohkin'? I manage apahtments an' people, dey mooveen out, all da time. Leave a big mess fo' me too. You help me wit da messes, I pay you $15 an hour, huh? You got a buddy? Good fo' two-man job da summah time."

I am actually looking for a job, and this *is* quite opportune. Banks has picked up a few shifts bartending, but he would probably be into it. "Yeah, man, why not? I'm looking for ways to pick up some extra money right now."

Ali'i looks over at me after taking a significant drag off his 120 Pall Mall, then flicking the ash out into the wind, "I dabble in many t' ings, you let me know what type of stuff you used to doing, an' I see wat I can do."

"Yeah, as long as it's legal," is my tentative and now slightly suspicious reply. I wear my emotions on my sleeve when I'm not on *survival mode*, so the suspicion registers in my tone. I feel in zero danger, but my antennas are now perked for any overly dicey shit.

"Don't worry, bruddah. You ahready whirrring too much. I'm famous... da ho islan'. You gonna' see."

I'm not an idiot, and I see immediately that this guy is a bit shady. But who hasn't been a bit dubious that has ever made me a $100 or made me laugh my ass off? As long as I don't act stupid, he can't exploit me too much. I'm smart; I grew up in the streets. You can only turn the willing in a situation like this, I figure.

He probably hasn't seen a Haole boy hitchhiking in a while. He's understandably intrigued. If he's on some gay shit, I'll bounce. Can't blame him for trying, I am a pretty hot piece of ass. Like a cross between James Franco and Vince Vaughn, Swingers era Vince Vaughn, less stoned than James and even quicker and wittier than Vince. A true knighted swordsman of shit-talking, too. How could they not try? It's almost mean not to let them at least attempt. I've worked for gay guys before, and they *will* try. You just tell them firmly "no," and they'll put an extra $40 in your check at the end of the week so that the situation is forgotten.

In the 90s, people are not that *out*. Most gays are generally straight acting until they are comfortable around you. They lower their guard once they trust you're not a homophobe. If you are a 90s American male, you probably *are* homophobic. Either that or you act like one for fear of being labeled a "homo" yourself. The creepier types might drop the straight act if they think there's a chance you are a junky that's in too deep with Mr. Brown Tar, and you'd be *gay for pay*. This last option is why my antennas are on alert. I ain't tryin' to suck a cock for a hundred spot.

There might be a price, but it definitely would be a reasonably large pile of hundreds stacked on top of each other, not just one. And rent would have to be due yesterday, and it would have to be as feminine of a cock as possible. Ali'i's Hawaiian penis may fit that bill, but no, the agedness of his *pineapple poki-pole* would have defeminized it too much. I'm sorry, I need to see the $100,000 upfront, in my peripheral vision, *while* I'm sucking. And it would have to be, like, a super-feminine cock.

And I don't have to take the load; most chicks that have blown me to completion have sensed the flood coming and just, kind of, cranked out the blast by hand. Could I crank out the blast? Ok, so we have:

1- crank out the blast

2- 100k in view while I suck.

3- as girly of a dick as you can get. Maybe Jared Leto? He seems like he could afford it.

I am **not** a homophobe, and I'm *definitely* not gay—aside from the preconditions stated above. What do I have to worry about? Fuck it if the Hawaiian Elvis is trying to fuck me. I just won't drink any beers he gives me unless I open them myself.

The next night Ali'i, the possibly gay pimp, takes Banks and me to a Luau—our first one, unless you count the time back home when Moish Brenham, the Filipino power Jew, burst into a house party naked and dancing. He had nothing but a palm frond wrapped around his waist, another around his head, doing the hula to punk music.

Ali'i sits between us at the Luau, and we watch the greased up male dancers throw sticks up into the air, spinning and on fire. I look to Ali'i, and yes, he's looking at the greased bodies as everyone else looks at the twirling sticks above our heads. I don't have a problem with it; I just want to know what his angle might be here. The girls swivel their hips in the semi-sensual tradition of their grandmothers, as we gorge on various local delicacies and overly decorated rum drinks. Soon, we are served a hog that was recently buried on coals in the sand for 24 hours. Everyone is wearing an aromatic flower *Lei* and smiling at the exotic celebration before us.

At one point, the MC points to Ali'i. "Look at dis. We got a celebrity in da house heeyah. Big time radio guy! Ali'i!"

Everyone turns to us and claps at Ali'i as he stands to accept the adoration of the crowd. It looks as if this has happened to him before. He waves and points at them with his hairy knuckled finger guns. Some of the luau employees give Banks and me a look over, wondering what kind of "security detail" we might be working.

"Ain't dis great, guys? Everybody love us! You on da team," says Ali'i, thinking we're basic idiots, just because we're pretty.

After that, Banks senses that he's being sold off a bit cheaply if we are to be some sort of *non-sexual, companionship escorts*. After that, he decides to stick to bartending. It's understandable, and I guess that *is* what the arrangement was. This guy is such a character I don't even care. I gotta study him. He's a true original, straight out of an Elmore Leonard book. A *jack of all trades*, above *and* below the table.

Ali'i is acting ok, so I start painting units for him. I'll be up on a ladder, and he brings in a beer every half hour and just kind of stands there watching me. It's a bit weird, and after the day is done, I'm sitting in his living room eating some pizza. He casually says, "You watch pohn? You know, I produce couple pohn movies, nutting too big but we make some money off a dem. Maybe I can get you sohm wuhk. You got a big dick o' wat?"

It's hard to make me say, "Uhm..." but that's what I do.

"Porn? I don't know, Ali'i. I mean, I don't really have a porn dick, you know? It's definitely above medium. As someone once said, 'It's a grower, not a shower.' Let's put it that way. I have never had a lot of confidence in it as a *public figure,* I guess, is what I'm trying to say. Cameras have made it shrink before. In its fluffed form, it's incredible. Unfortunately, there are several other forms, none of which inspire terms such as 'mega-girth.'"

Ali'i is cracking up. "Ha-ha. You funny guy, J.C.! I never meet a Haole funny like you. Fucking crazy guy. Look. You gonna be fine. We gonna get you some tiny Asian girls. Hawaii got lots of tiny Asian girls. You gonna be huuuuge! Dey gonna say, 'Ruuunnnn! Godzeeeeella!!' Look, I'm gonna put in one of da movies. We can see if you tink you can do it, ok?"

"You *made* this one? Don't fucking lie, Ali'i! The only reason I would watch a porn with another guy is if **he** directed it. You know, to form a review of the artistic merits."

"Yeah, I make it. Don't worry, I'm not da staaah. I'm holding da camera an' I pay da money fo da actahs and da' quipment. No pay fo studio doh. We make it in da room you paint yestahday."

"Are you shitting me? Of course, you're not."

"Ha-ha-ha-ha-ha!" Ali'i really lets one out.

Then he pops in an old VHS copy of his self-made flesh film, no visible title on the tape itself. The first wavy bands of the tapes pre-cum wear themselves out, and we are instantly at a scene that does indeed appear to have been filmed in the room I painted yesterday. A blonde lady is sucking off the cock of a blond man as he cranks her ponytail towards the base of his churning boner. Then, in an unexpected turn of events, a brown-haired guy with jailhouse tats on his forearms comes into the room and says, "What the fuck are you doing, **whore**?!"

He seems surprised, but he's naked as well. *Was he just like that? Arriving home unexpectedly and buck naked?* Odd. I slightly demerit the film in my mind at this glaring oversight. Then the blonde and bored housewife says, "Nothing, baby, I was just saving you a surprise."

Next thing you know, the *cuckholdee* has grabbed the *cuckholder* and flips him over for a look at his *puckered sockeye*. It seems to be in tip-top shape because the next thing you know, it's being stuffed with a surgically enhanced pork tenderloin. *Where did the blonde chick even go?* The fact that Ali'i sat next to me on the couch after putting in the tape instead of the perfectly comfortable Lazy Boy recliner two-feet away is also a bit concerning.

"Whoah, Ali'i. Not cool dude. This shit is not my type of porn! I barely can look at anal even if it's a chick getting it. It's barbaric. And I got no problem if you're gay, Ali'i, but *I'm* definitely not."

"Gay?! I'm not gay. Wat da fuck you say?!"

Ali'i is flustered for the first time in my presence, mad even. Maybe he's *not* gay. Perhaps I shouldn't have said that. Usually, when an older male stranger picks you up hitchhiking, wants to spend time with you, and take care of you, he's gay. This would be a first, but sure, it's possible…I guess. "I'm sorry. I wasn't accusing you, but, I mean, you just put on gay porn and sat down next to me, that's all." I stand up to signal I'm leaving soon and so that I can crack this motherfucker in the head if he gets wacky on me.

"Aaah, bruddah. I don't keep a big selection of da movies aroun' heeyah. My muddah gohn visit. Evy munt she come ovah. 85 yeahs ole. I cannot have a box a pohn sitting on da shelf," Ali'i counters.

"Ok, that's fine. Let me think about it, Ali'i."

I manage to leave the situation a bit less awkward than it was when the porn scene revealed its adulterous plot twist. I go down to the beach and think about how much money would I require to do this. Ali'i promised no gay shit, just me and two tiny Asian girls. I sit on the beach, mesmerized by the blinking rails of sun reflected in the small waves as they break, thinking it over.

Sitting there, I imagine what I would want the movie to go like. There's me, the two Japanese girls, my cock is all pre-fluffed and shiny from the pre-shoot coconut oil greasing. We're there, in the jacuzzi, popping a bottle of Dom Perignon. I'm about to get revenge for Pearl Harbor on their pussies. But wait! Ali'i did some last-second script rewrites! All of a sudden, a giant Samoan, kicks through the thin partition wall with a baseball bat and charges me, yelling, "Welcome to yo snuff film, bruddah!!!"

>>Jolted back to reality!<< Now I have to go home and possibly find Razor hanging from the rafters. I take a two-block detour around Ali'i's house.

Coconut Fisticuffs

Banks and I find a cheap place and sign a six-month lease. That day, we go out and celebrate by buying a fifth of rum and a two-liter of Coke. We drink it on a curb in a parking lot. People just sit anywhere in Hawaii, it doesn't matter, you just walk until you get too hot, and you just sit down wherever that happens to be.

Later, we find out there is a keg party in the apartment complex we just moved into. We decide to go over there with our buddies, Ritchie and Stevie. We settle in and get a beer at the keg that's populated by what looks like 18–23yo kids, most of which look fresh off the boat from Laguna Beach.

After we get our keg cups filled, Ritchie and Stevie tell us they got jumped by these three local kids that are there. After we have a few and the other kids have a few, some insults start getting thrown the way of Stevie and Ritchie. I, of course, have to try to be the peacemaker. Too bad no one told me there's no peacemaking in Hawaii. If it's on, it's on. So, Banks becomes a sudden diplomat as well and provokes the anger of two identical twin Hawaiian hooligan instigators. Stevie and Ritchie are these two 19yo kids that clearly don't want anything to do with this bullshit. That's about how old the Hawaiian twins are, but they are more muscular and angrier.

They want to fight and head straight for Banks. I take out the first kid with a hook to the jaw, and he goes down like a sack of bricks! Then his identical twin brother—no shit—jumps out of the crowd at me, and I clock *him* down to the ground as well. They're both on the ground at once like a tragic *Double Mint* commercial. The whole party of Laguna kids pile up behind the local kids in anticipation of us getting our asses kicked. So that's when I decide the gang and I should retreat. I don't know if I can take them *and* their friend, who had backed up a bit when he saw what happened to his buddies. Now he's jumping up and doing roundhouse kicks at head level, putting on a real karate exhibition. Banks, as we've talked about, isn't much of a fighter, and from the looks on Ritchie and Stevie's faces? I can safely guess that I'm on my own here. Fuck it. "Let's get the fuck out of here!" I yell.

I am off and running, thinking I'm leading the charge to get a drink at Hecock's. I stop to see what's behind me a few blocks later, and there's nothing. No Banks, no Ritchie, no Stevie! *Nada.* I sidetrack one block over to Ritchie and Stevie's house, and that's where I find them. Banks isn't here. "Where the fuck is Banks?!" I scream like a scary madman.

"Banks stayed and tried to talk to them, and they hit him!" says Ritchie.

"What?!"

I grab a butcher knife out of their kitchen and run back to the party. Banks and the Hawaiian kids aren't there. I visualize them and Banks in a car on the way to the pineapple fields. Much later, I discover Banks is in the house we just moved into 20 yards away. Meanwhile, the Hawaiian kids are going and getting some of their older, larger uncles. It looks like people are still getting beer out of the keg, and they become somewhat agitated that I've returned.

I lunge back down the block, thinking maybe they decided on the more practical method of taking Banks down to the beach where they can blend his tortured gurglings in with the rolling surf. I get down to the beach, and Banks isn't being killed there either.

I go to Hecock's, thinking perhaps he got away and went there. I order a drink and ask the bartender, Stan, if he's seen him. He hasn't, so I down my shot of whiskey and hit the street looking for him with a butcher knife still in my shorts. And then I see them, a small VW Rabbit filled with angry locals, pointing angrily in my direction. Oh shit!

I turn around and sprint away as if I can outrun a car or something. I can hear them yelling, a few heads pop out the windows *Pop!! Pop!!* Go the shots in the night!

Oh shit, they're trying to kill me!—It sounds like one of them is shooting a low caliber gun at me—*What the fuck is happening right now?!*

I dodge right, towards the beach where I just came from and manage to get on an unlit passage to the sand as one of the cars unloads for a Haole fox hunt! I trip, trying to take a sharp angle as I reach the sand, cartwheeling and losing the knife. I sense someone 30-yards back in the darkness. It's a dark, sliver mooned night. I manage to get to the beach at Lahaina Shores Hotel. I'm spotted coming into the lighted pool area— the same pool I had jumped into from the balcony just weeks before. This security guy is going to be pretty upset to see me again, I'm guessing.

I run into the hotel lobby and race up to the concierge desk. There is a lady there, and I look into her eyes and think. *This woman will help me.* "Lady! You gotta help me. They're going to kill me!"

I jump over the lady's 4-foot tall counter and land about two-inches from where she's sitting. She doesn't flinch like I thought she might. I hide in the tiny, doorless office behind her. There's a folding metal chair, which I fold up and crouch as tightly and defensively as I can up against the wall. I think in my head with adrenaline clarity, *Ok! Hit the gun, get the gun and maybe you can live!*

Then the guys come running into the lobby and right up to the counter! I assume they saw me jump the counter, and I prepare for the moment. *Alright, bring it on then!* I grip the chair and raise it above my head.

"Where is he? You saw him run through!" they yell at the lady at the desk.

She doesn't say anything right off the bat, and I'm thinking, *Shit! She's gonna rat me out! She's gonna rat me out! They probably have a gun pointed at her!!*

She doesn't. "He ran out the front," she mercifully lies.

And so, in a miracle of miracles, they run out the front! This lady is a saint! Unfortunately, there is a whole other car out in front, and they tell the disembarked brawlers that I haven't come that way. They say I 'must still be in the hotel.' So, they run back in the lobby, and they are *really* threatening to her this time. Again, she tries to get rid of them. All the while, I'm like, *This lady has got some grit! Thank god I ran in here!* I am afraid they're going to hear my heart beating and shoot me through the drywall, but the lady gets rid of them again. I don't budge because

I am not sure if they are watching her through the glass or what. So I stay put for a little while.

About ten minutes later, someone comes into the office. I lower the chair, seeing it's not one of the hooligans. Still, I entertain the thought that this guy is one of the local kids' uncles, and I'm still going to wind up face down in the pineapple patch. I can see, in the partially dark room, this guy isn't a local, he's Italian or something. *Wait. It's the same rent-a-cop that told me to stop jumping off the balcony a few weeks ago.* No one has ever been happier to see a possibly–Italian rent–a–cop! "Kid? You're just here on vacation, right?! Because you should leave. It's a small town here."

"Yeah, my plane leaves tomorrow, trust me. Will you call me a cab?" I say.

"Yeah, okay. Don't come back here. I know you're the guy fro—"

"I won't, trust me, call me a cab, and I won't even come on this whole street again," I beseech the police academy drop out. I'm still worried these guys are just circling.

So, the guy calls a cab, and I wait there.

As I'm leaving, I go to thank the lady, and she averts her eyes from shyness or annoyance. Maybe I embarrassed her by making her a hero. "Thank you so much, ma'am. You're a saint! I was just trying to be a Good Samaritan like you, and it went bad. I swear."

"Oh, I'm sure it had a little bit to do with your drinking, I could smell it when you blew by me," she replies with a faint smile.

"It was more their fault! Like way more!" I counter, not jumping over hers this time.

"Ok, I'll believe that," she says, as she looks at me through her glasses and blonde bangs. She's about 45 with a convinced, reserved morality about her. She seems like a slice of middle American pie, magically transported in time and space just in time to save a ho. I'm happy she said she believes that it was more their fault. I know she won't take any external credit for what she did, but I like to think that deep down inside, she's a little proud of standing those boys down for a stranger.

I have never been that big of a hero for someone before—I saved Allen Sun from getting thrown off the Isla Vista cliffs once, but I think I was just delaying destiny there—I always try to fix up street urchins with a shower, a pep talk, and something to eat. Still, here, this humble lady has saved my entire life, and she isn't even trying to rub it in. *What a great lady!* "You're a great lady!" I say as I walk out the front door into a cab after giving the street an eyeball check.

"How's your night going, buddy?" says the cabbie.

"A little bit crazy. Will you take me to Waine'e Street?"

So, off to the house I moved into yesterday, and now I'm moving out of tomorrow. Banks is there with Kel, worried *I* was the one face down in the pineapple fields, but not so much that he ever left the apartment complex. I tell them how the rest of my night went. It seems like the Maui Mafia is going to be hunting for me if I stick around. Painting units for Ali'i didn't exactly add up, and I've been here for five months trying to make it happen. Fuck it. I'm ready to go home. Within eight hours, I'm back on Oahu, having escaped being shot down in the street by some angry Samoans.

I find Shipley's Ale House and Grill to be in full swing. For a few days, I'm living high on the hog, telling my story of survival, eating prawns, garlic mashed potatoes, all types of fishes, and drinking Jack and Cokes. Soon, I head back to the mainland. Thanks, Hawaii. You were interesting, but fuck you. I am not trying to die out here on this obscure, isolated, lava rock bullshit.

A Legal Paycheck

How do I cash this fuckin' thing? After returning from Hawaii with my tail between my legs, I had decided to make a concerted effort to get a real job here in Santa Barbara. I decided it was time to grow up at the ripe age of 24. Alexander the Great had probably already taken over at least several islands by this age. Yet, here I am, still screwing around with keg party fights and bipolar girls who leave bites.

It's 1997, Bill Clinton just won a second term. In response, the brutalized Republicans launch the Fox News channel. Michael Jordan and the Bulls are on their second three-peat, the radio is playing shit like The Macarena and Wonderwall, people have cell phones now. Girls all seem to be wearing sundresses that they need little provocation to tear off and reveal their teeny bikinis. Men, the slovenly pieces of shit they are, respond with cargo shorts and Tevas. Except for the sundresses, things are going downhill quick, culturewise. My cute teenage, "Hey, can I crash on your couch for a week?" shit doesn't seem to have its old *razzle-dazzle*. It was a good run, old boy, but it's time to make a few concessions to The Man.

After I've completed training and an additional week of work as a trusted decaf latte preparer for the soccer moms of State Street, I finally receive my payroll check. I promptly rip it, trying to work the thick perforations protecting my social security number from people I used to be like.

I've been alerted by my boss and Coffee Bean and Tea Leaf franchise owner, Linda, that we are indeed in the most expensively rented shop per square foot between Beverly Hills and San Francisco. What that means is that it is imperative to be efficient and well-groomed at all times. Profit loss is no joke and must be prevented no matter the discomfort it may cause me as I obligatorily and convincingly smile through the pain. That, among many other requirements, is mentioned in the thick employee handbook I will be taking a written quiz on later.

Linda pauses for me to digest the million things that just fell out my other ear. She is a short, stout lady with well-conditioned grey hair and piercing eyes that look like they see everything through her horn-rimmed glasses. In a gesture of comradery, Linda also wears the official Coffee Bean and Tea Leaf, *shit brown* apron that we all sport. I tell her that I will protect her investment. As soon as she turns her back, I promptly begin punching out, at ten punches per card, free ice-blended mochas to hand out to all the pretty girls that work in the hundreds of retail shops that branch out into the retail powerhouse that is downtown Santa Barbara. I figure having a bunch of model types hanging out in the store drinking free blended coffee drinks will lead to less profit loss and turn me into a **boss** of ass.

During business hours, I lay directly in the middle of this hen house of wonder muff, with all the different free ice coffees and berried Arnold Palmers a girl could ever want.

It's going to be a good year no matter what I have to do. This is the year of re-building. No whiskey, no cocaine. Weed, beer, and sex only. I've changed—and just in time, according to modern maturity standards—If you're not driving a truck with a company logo stickered onto the door by the time you're 26, then forget about it.

Girls in their mid-20s downtown are far different than the college sophomores of UCSB. They have requirements. You must have showered today, have a job, *and* a room with a mattress—that is up on a frame! At that point, she may allow you to take her to a restaurant, which must have metal forks and knives, where she will consider sleeping with you if you are funny enough and don't try to make her pay half. "Oh, I'm funny enough, but are you going to order another glass of wine? Because I'm doing some counting in my head, and I might have to stiff the nice waiter if you do."

It's a jacked-up system, but if you want the tender female touch of a non-coke head, non-bar skank, non-halitosis carrier, then you have to play it. I have to stop reeling in broken chicks out of the dive bars. The last one? I lifted her dress and she was wearing an abortion diaper. She had gotten an abortion that weekend, and there were pieces of the baby the tongs didn't get. They were now leaking into this, like, diaper. She's already out hunting for more dick still wearing her motherfucking post-abortion diaper. Truly unethical and frankly gross. This discovery makes my penis shrivel inwards like a stepped-on tide pool creature.

I think I need a plan to vet these girls a little better. Perhaps a short quiz with questions like: "Do you have Harley Davidson posters in your room?" "How many pit-bulls are likely to be on the couch?" "Do you have a mostly stamped out punch card for Planned Parenthood?"

With steady income coming in, I've found a humble living situation. I'm living with Ozzy, the guy who pissed on me when he was sleepwalking, "allegedly," at Laduska's house seven years ago. It's a quaint, well odored from the dogs of yesteryear's past, creaking board apartment on De la Vina and Anapamu. $400 a month to live in the living room. It's a start.

It has been more than three years since I broke up with my first girlfriend. It's time to clean myself up and get another good woman so we can just watch Blockbuster movies on the couch. Make spaghetti dinners at her house and stay out of the bars. Call me Domestic Donnie from now on—just me and Marine Biologist Margaret over here! This is the dream I have, to just be normal for a little while and rest.

And that's why you can now find me searching for the face of a lady I no longer remember. It's mostly the same blonde framed faces as the rest of the sea of working professionals interspersed with the previously mentioned soccer moms, all of them eagerly staring at me in anticipation of their caffeinated lunches.

"Pardon me, ma'am. Would you like whipped cream on that decaf, non-fat, half vanilla, half chocolate, ice-blended mocha?"

I scan for a look of acknowledgment from any one of them. "Yes!" half of them respond at once.

"A little bit," goes a straggler.

It's not the life of a playboy, but I feel proud. I feel like I have been let into a door that was previously locked to me in downtown Santa Barbara, the door of *gainful employment*. Perhaps my notoriety hasn't permeated the daytime crowd yet. After all, I never get crazy until after midnight, and these suckers are probably sleeping by then. I never thought of that. This could work!

I will learn from these people, as I was unable to from my father, how to get along in society without being a short-lived pirate. It could be nice. A pregnant wife sitting in our yard, the dog barking at a hummingbird that is sucking the syrupy sap out of perfectly trimmed bird of paradise bushes. Tomahawk steaks sizzling on a BBQ. Health insurance. Fuck it. Is that too much to ask? I deserve a good life. Why not?

Apparently, it is too much to ask. Once I start cashing those paychecks, the wads of cash are just burning a hole in my pocket. Soon, I am back in the dive bars buying people shots who wouldn't bail me out of jail if it was a nickel. I show up to work looking rough every Sunday for a few months, and I think Linda catches wind of my card stamping scam.

Soon, I get caught on camera dipping down below the register to inhale nitrous hits out of the emptied whip cream cans. Empty of everything but the sweet, air heady nitrous high known as "hippy crack." Oopsy. I figure if there's a rare minute when there are no customers, I should be able to spend a little break however I want. According to the official Coffee Bean and Tea Leaf handbook? No. It clearly says "No" on that on pages 12 and 46-48. I am made aware of this fact by a furious Linda, who once freaked out on an employee for saying our products give you a buzz.

"You make it sound like a narcotic!" she spazzedly screamed.

I should have foreseen this scenario. Linda shakily hands me my final check, and that's that. Oh well. The dive bars are calling. I guess I should just accept myself for what I am. A whiskey-pirate whose ship is made out of cocaine.

Hidden Camera Show
of the Crueler Gods

As if this isn't all too much, one of my best friends, Kit, dies after hitting his head skateboarding. Kit was getting ready to tape a part in a professional skate video. The pressure to go bigger than you have ever gone is incredible for these videos. He misjudged his landing by an inch or two and went flying into something headfirst. He complained of a headache later in the evening and just keeled over dead. The sweetest guy you could ever meet, always asking people how they were doing and trying to encourage them, even though most of the time, he didn't have two pieces of sourdough to rub together himself. As long as he had a skateboard and concrete to flip, grind, and jump around on, he didn't care about shit. He was always smiling and laughing. Bad moods just dissolved around him. Confident wherever he went, he just was one of the *best* ones.

Why is it always the dope motherfuckers? I'm in such a shitty state in my own life right now. I would totally trade myself for him. He was doing something. He had gone pro at skating, and he was living his dreams out the exact way he wanted. And here I am, brutally reduced, but still too much alive. I guess if you are born with a high tolerance for pain, it's because you're destined to rub that brake pad until the sparks fly.

I feel like Shame and Tragedy are both sitting on my chest, and I can't breathe. If I try to gasp, they shit in my mouth and laugh. I want to destroy everything, including myself. I continue to drink and snort my way through the agony. The short windows of the late evening, where I feel almost pain-free, grow smaller and smaller every week. I cry openly in the bar for a few days after the news, and people still come up to me to buy coke, which I sell to them, no break in the tears, and the wet chest heaves.

How have I become such a broken man in such a short time? Because it hasn't been a short time. Since I broke up with Shawna, it has been over three years of this endless festival of torment with light breaks in between. You've got to shake it off, dude. You might be an immortal motherfucker, but there are worse things than being dead. I'm going to come out of this like a Vietnam vet that was in the shit too long, and now he has just two gears in his emotional Rolodex: *dead inside/ homicidally enraged.* Being drunk and high is the only time I'm not miserable during this period.

Kit's Benefit

It's the morning of Kit's benefit in San Francisco, where he died and was doing most of his skating these days. I wake up late, hungover as fuck and miss all the rides up north. *Shit. I cannot miss this. Fuck.* I slowly drag myself towards the nearest freeway exit at Carrillo Street, headed North on the 101. It's a good exit to hitch if you are desperate. The gravy filled hitchhiking days of the hippies have gone as extinct as the hippies themselves have gone politically moderate. However, I'm no ordinary hitchhiker, and as the cars pass, I psychically make them look over at me and make split-second eye contact. It's all the time I need to raise my eyebrows in a "Hey, I got weed," or, "Hey, I don't stink and won't talk too much." All three of these things are lies, but I need a fuckin' ride.

Here comes a truck. *Yes!* It's Gabe, the doorman at one of the bars I frequent. He's pretty smart and funny as doormen go, and he likes to party. Last time I saw him at a house party, he threw some other jocks in the pool. People love it when bullies get bullied, even if it's another bully doing the bullying. He is going up to Cal Poly University to visit some girl. That's a third of the way to San Francisco—and I barely had my thumb out!

"Damn, Gabe. Are you driving up to a different area code for a piece of ass? You don't strike me like the pussy whippable kind. I guess even guys with muscles got feelings, huh?"

"Ok, now I'm charging you gas money," Gabe says.

"Whoa, whoa. I'm just kidding. A little light humor for the road ahead, that's all."

"Are the sheriff's going to pull me over if they see you in this truck? Are we escaping the city limits right now? I could have brought the white Bronco."

"Nah, I'm not even holding. I haven't had a warrant in years, dude," I say while checking the side view mirror for potential creeping lobbers.

About a third of the way there, I get dropped off by that big steep volcanic looking mountain by Cal Poly, in San Luis Obispo. I have my thumb out for about a half-hour, but it seems like an hour. Hitchhiking sucks, and I got spoiled on that first ride. I make eye contact with a cowboy-hatted Mexican. There are two of them. I could tell he would have picked me up, but he saw me too late. *Shit.* A few minutes later, these same guys come pulling up in a rusty cream-colored sedan. I get in the back, and I say, "You guys passed me up a minute ago. Why did you go to so much trouble? I mean, thanks, but..."

One of the Cowboy hats spins to the side, and I see the kind, chubby, goateed face say, "Dios say."

Well then. Like, Dios says just to do that shit? Or, like a spirit came in this car and told you to turn around? Because that might have been Kit. Maybe his curly hair was backlit by the sun and looked like a halo? This would be a splendid time to have gotten off my ass a few years ago and learned Spanish.

They are going all the way to San Francisco. What a score! I'm going to make it with an hour to spare. We stop at Denny's in King City, and when I try to stay in the car, they make me come in and buy me some food. I am embarrassed because I'm out of my element, and I feel more somber than brash due to the circumstances of the trip. Plus, these guys have picked me up as if it were some sort of Blues Brothers' spiritual mission. I don't want to put any type of stink on that. At .04% body fat, I'm in no position to turn down the stockpile of carbs, animal fat, protein, and caffeine that a trip into Denny's would provide.

I get chicken fried steak with cream gravy, crispy hash browns, and a biscuit. Add to that a bottomless coffee, and I'm good for this whole trip. By the last three bites, I'm almost sick, but my *feast or famine* instincts force the bites down. After that, I'm ready to go curl up in the backseat for the rest of the ride.

When we get into The City, it's dark. I get dropped off in South Market, towards the end between the Ferry Building and the Oakland Bridge. I'm looking for the Maritime Hall. That's all I know, along with the general area. I realize that I am in a sort of desolate part of town and start to panic that I might not find it after all this. *Shit.* My life is a series of *shits!* And *fucks!* All of a sudden, as I'm about to sit on the curb, here comes Tom Estes, slowing up alongside me in the back of a Yellow Cab. "You want a ride, Lurker?"

"Fuck, yes! Am I glad to see you!" I can't believe it. It's as if when I missed all the rides, the spirit of Kit was like, *"Oh shit!"* and he carried me in his hand. Thanks, Kitster!

Next thing you know, we're walking inside the venue. It's huge. They've built a halfpipe to the right of the stage, and all the best pro-skaters are pulling huge airs while the Santa Barbara band Lagwagon plays. They are shredding to the glee of the mashing tornado pit before them. 7-foot-tall Chris Flippin, slaying the guitar as 5-foot Joey Cape, looking like a thimble beside him, shouts his raspy helium voice into the mic in poppy, punk verses that are funnily worded, melodic and playful. Great for parties.

They have some albums out now on Fat Wreck Chords, NOFX's label. Lagwagon is another Santa Barbara band getting their due, having too much fun to try and get too famous. Maybe that's the smart way to go. They did turn down some offers on some more prominent labels, it's true. The headliners always seem to be the most miserable and drug-addicted ones anyway. These are great guys that I know from a million other SB and Goleta bands that I saw play on hundreds of weekends growing up. Kit would be happy they're headlining his memorial. Right on!

I feel Kit's spirit in the building, nodding in approval. He's probably laughing and saying shit like, "Sweet rager!" "Where's the keg at?" "Who has that ganny gib?!" "Light it up! Don't hide it, divide it!" "Hey, ladies! Ditch the squid and get with The Kid!" "Ha! This is fuckin' DOPE!!!" "Seriously, though, **spark it up!**"

I look around and see that I missed a lot of rides. Even Hanglo managed to make it 325 miles without getting two DUIs. At one point, I meet Kit's mom, who looks exactly like him. She is tall and rabbit-like, with curly blonde hair, freckly skin, and a kind face. Missing the glint in the eye Kit used to always have. Always ready for mischief, a skate session, sometimes both at once. You can hardly blame her for missing the glint, due to the circumstances of the occasion. God, if I look at her one more second, I'm going to lose it. She looks just like him.

They play on a projector, 40-feet high on the wall, a video of Kit skating, and talking. I'm standing there, with Brandon Chapman, Kit's mom, Laduska, G-Money, and Kristen, the last girl I knew to have dated Kit. When we hear Kit's voice talking on the projected video, that's it for all of us. I start bawling until tears drip into my socks. I just can't believe it. Kit was supposed to live forever, that sweet boy who always tried to cheer people up or make them laugh. It's me, John O'Brien or Hanglo that were supposed to die. The crazy ones. Why do the good ones get taken? This is a huge loss for the power of good. I can't take it. I am so comforted to see this grand celebration of his life. To be in this big room with so many that felt the same way about him as I did. It's fucking unfathomable. I have got to go cry.

Apple Sauce

I've set up shop on De La Guerra and Castillo Streets at Scott's house. There are several couches I can crash on within a three-block radius to give his roommates enough of a break from me as to not make a ban attempt for a while. It's close to State Street, Elsie's Bar, and The Wildcat. Scott's is where I end up if I can't find a dive bar girl to take me home and feed me spaghetti. Also, I have a foam mat stashed in the yard if the door is locked when I get done drinking. There's no way I can fail around here—Oh yeah, did I mention the dive bars got me back, and I missed rent at Ozzie's house? Ooopsie.

One night, I'm next door on the porch at Vespa Jason's house with Scott and his cousin Troy. We're all yacked out beyond belief on coke, and Scott is on one of his *conspiracy theory ramperbants* about chemtrails or some shit.

Just when we're about to throw him over the balcony, the girls who just moved in across the street walk by, and they invite Jason and me up for a bong hit. They are very particular that it's only Jason and me they want to come over. "Our living room is super tiny," they explain.

I guess they heard Scott ranting into oblivion and could tell by the look on Troy's face that he'd be an intellectual burden. So, just Jason and I gladly go over to their house, up the stairs where we take bong hits in a room that looks right down onto Jason's balcony. We can still see Scott excitedly *gibble-gabbling* as if working his jawbone releases orgasms.

It's a polite session with no sexual vibe, which is fine, and soon we're crossing the street back towards the balcony. As we're coming up the stairs, Scott is all, "Oh my god, did you fuck 'em?! Did you just fuck 'em?!"

Jason starts to answer, and I grab his shoulder to cut him off. I have a brilliant idea. As their eyes bug out in anticipation of some detailed vaginal descriptions, I say to Scott and Troy, "Yeah, we fucked 'em! And they were so hot we got excited, and we came too quick, and they said to send you guys over to finish the job. Oh my god, my girl was so tight I thought it wasn't going to work, but we finally got it in. Didn't you hear the screams? She's trippin' bro."

"No, we didn't hear anything," says Troy.

"Really? Oh, man. I thought my girl was going to claw my back off. She was ready!" says Jason, quickly catching on to the ruse.

Scott is so coked up he would believe any fairy tale as long as it ends with him getting pussy. He's ready to pull out his wiener right now and start priming it. "What?! WHICH APARTMENT?!?! WHERE?!"

"Well, it's that lit up window right there," I point. Now, I've had time to invent the rest of the prank.

One of the girls is standing visibly in it, which causes a slight, jerky,

Gollumesque gurgle in Scott's throat. A gurgle which tells me he almost came just seeing a girl he thinks might want to fuck him. I know this will be easy. I could send him off on nearly any adventure. Scott and Troy start charging out of the yard.

"Wait. You guys, you see that crabapple tree right there?"—I remembered kicking through a few crabapples that had fallen on the ground as we went through their yard both ways—"They for sure want you guys to come over, but the buzzer is broken. They said to pick up the apples off the ground and throw them up at the window, and when they open it, you have to yell the code word, *"Apple sauce."*

Scott and Troy don't even question the absurdity of this. The next thing you know, they are across the street throwing apples up at these poor girls' windows. Sure enough, the window opens, and these dumb fucks start yelling, "Applesauce! Applesauce!" at the mystified young women up there.

Jason and I are starting to lose it, as we have a perfect view of the entire episode. The girls give each other an annoyed look. One pokes her head down at them and yells, "Get the fuck out of our yard, you fuckin' idiots. We're calling the cops!" before slamming the window shut.

The guys come back across the street, confused, and once they see Jason and me rolling on the ground laughing, they finally realize they've been had. "Fuckin' idiots," is right.

Now that, my friends, is how you turn a night from a lame thing to an amazing thing. I will never forget the sad look on their stupid faces once they realized I screwed them. Ha-ha. *Apple Sauce.* Who the fuck uses *that* as a code word?

Boxing for Dollars

One day, Brian Smallers says to me, "J.C., I think you're the biggest loudmouth in town, and I'm tired of waiting to see if someone's gonna punch you out. I got this guy, and you're going to box him in my back yard. I'll build a ring and everything."

"What's the cash prize?" I ask, trying to sound indifferent.

"$150," Brian decides as if he's already thought about it a bit.

"Alright, as long as the guy isn't like 50 pounds bigger than me."

"No, no," says Brian, reassuringly.

It turns out, he's only 40 pounds bigger than me, and his father trained him to box in Mexico. The guy is in shape from working 12 hours of hard labor every day. The only chink in his armor is he smokes a pack a day. I don't find any of this out until the event, so it's too late to do the pushups I might have done yesterday. I'll be boxing Brian's landscaping slave. Brian has what he calls a "landscaping business," where he drops off Andres with a lawnmower and some hedge clippers, goes and surfs, then takes half the money. Whatever of the money that doesn't go up his nose goes to gas for his shitty truck and the ancient lawnmower. Maybe a trip to Cuca's for a super-steak burrito. A lot of these surfer-ass looking dudes trying to come off like The Dude are actually a lot closer to Pauly Shore in his real-life, spoiled So-Cal coke heads that would be nowhere without mommy.

Brian does build a more official-looking ring than I thought he would. He's pounded in cheap metal fence stakes into his driveway, the ones that have the metal arrows sticking up from the bottom. They are dangerous and completely exposed. I make him tie carpet and foam rubber around them, and the rope is just regular nylon, but all in all, I'm impressed. He has gloves but no tape, a referee in a fake tuxedo t-shirt, a bell dinger, and judges.

I believe the judge booth is polluted, but I don't care, it won't come down to a decision anyway. It's gonna come down to who is laying down and who is still standing. Also, there are about 40 spectators here. This thing is on. To show just how macho I am, right up until they lace up the gloves on us, I've got a beer in my hand, and I'm sucking cigarettes down into my shallow breathing cocaine lungs.

My bravado must psych him out a little because when the bell rings, I walk right up to him and smack him full fledge in the head with months of pent up frustration all exploding out at once. Judging from the sound and the way his head cocks back, I think I kill him. Not even close. He's only sort of fucked up. In the next round, I proceed to pummel him, and his eyes are looking scared. Fuck this. I'm going for the knockout on the next bell ding!

I throw a Conan blow, but it bounces awkwardly off his now sweaty head and only throws a small ripple through his face. I feel pain shoot through my untaped fingers. He keeps going, I know I'm hurting him, but the kid is big. He won't fall. I am hitting him with every ounce of hatred in my body, and I don't even really know him. I certainly don't hate him in real life. I don't even *see* his face. Over it, I superimpose all those who have caused me embarrassment, laughed at, or caused me suffering. They all blink up in turn, all of my enemies throughout my life: the cops that tore down my mom's teepee, the people who keep calling me Lurk in front of cute girls, even after I turned 18, and it wasn't my nickname anymore. I think of the winters as a kid freezing in some unlocked car trying to sleep in the backseat wishing I had a blanket or at least a bigger jacket, wondering if the sun would ever come up again—and where is my sister and brother? are they freezing too?—I let the memories freeze my heart. Every time I hit him, I do it as if he's piling ice cubes onto my shivering siblings.

Andres still won't fall, he's too big. These gloves are bullshit. I'm fighting him like we're in a street brawl using elbows and headlocks. I'm trying to kill the guy. By the fourth round, I'm all punched out, and he starts landing a couple blows.

The fight goes from exciting to embarrassing in one round. We are both tired and looking sloppy. The crowd is starting to get mean. "Hit him in his fuckin' head! Smack him!" they scream.

"Why are they moving like that?" Dana says to her high school sweety, Spurwell.

"They're getting tired, babe," he says, killing my already quickly fading confidence.

Motormouth Scotty, worst corner coach ever, asks me, "You want me to throw in the towel?"

"Fuck, no!" I say threateningly through a scowl.

Hanelslap is there, and his expression has gone from excitement to disappointment and concern. The worst.

The bell rings again. I fake a right, and when he ducks, I come in with the uppercut with *lefty*, looking to end the fight with the last of what I have. I come in smoking and again get a bad bounce off his head. Not having tape on my hands, my pinky knuckle explodes. I take off the glove and lay down to cradle my little bitch finger, and by the time I get up, everyone I know has pretty much left. I didn't get to tell them, "It was my knuckle! Look! Find some tape! I'll keep fighting."

Motormouth Scotty is still there. I now see the white towel he threw into the ring. That pretty much says it all. All I am worried about is what people were thinking as they were leaving. And it struck me that I never used to care what people thought about anything. But now here I am, looking around for someone to show my knuckle to. What a bitch.

I'm sorry if this story is anticlimactic, but the point is that sometimes, life is a street fight, and you have to go in with everything you have and end it quickly. And other times, life puts gloves on you, and you've got to do the dance for a while.

Ok, that's not the point. The point is, I needed that loss. I needed to be humbled and made to realize that I am fucking up. I'm sleeping in people's yards for Christ's sake and acting like a drunk jackass all the time with less and less poetry and finesse. People think this shit is way less cute downtown than in the college town I half-assedly reared myself in. It's a town full of partyers, but there is a limit, and I'm pushing it.

Taco Fell

One night up on The Mesa, we are at the Cliff Room, making the bartender laugh. I forget who I was with, probably Motormouth. They are pouring giant shots for us until we can't even keep the balls on the pool table. We wander around outside smoking cigs, and we see a Taco Bell with a late-night, walk-up order window. When we get up to the front, this skinny little City College freshman in basketball shorts is ordering the whole menu and asking all kinds of questions about the food.

I'm annoyed. "Dude, it's Taco Bell! It's all variations of cheese, meat, rice, beans, and tortilla! Sometimes the tortilla is soft, and sometimes it's crispy. That's the only curveball!"

He pretends not to hear me and continues ordering one of everything, taking long pauses while he ponders the menu like the Sunday Crossword.

"Oh, what the fuck?" I can't take it anymore. I shove him through the order window into the restaurant, pulling his shorts down to his ankles as he drops to the floor. We run away laughing before the poor employees can identify us, deciding to come back later, after another shot or two.

Around this time, I walk into Brian Lee, a fancy men's boutique specializing in high priced denim. The owner takes one look at me and says, "Oh, the horror." I guess I look like I feel. When you crawl out of a mysterious couch into the hateful daylight, you should at least take a little slut spritz in the bathroom sink before you steal a bagel out of the kitchen and bounce. The youthful freshness that has allowed me to float on my derelict behavior and still be considered pleasant to look at is now getting a bit stale. Dana, from the boxing match, the girl I'm there to say "Hi." to, is like, "Jesus, J.C., you are an embarrassment right now. Go take a shower someplace and come back later. I'm buying you an outfit." Ouch. Call me an asshole, but ugly? That's a new one. My good looks are all I have ever been able to count on besides this silver tongue.

After that, I reduce the partying until I fall from the upper echelon to the middle of the alcoholic cokehead crowd. Still a lot of room for creativity there. I find a steady crash spot where I can have some clean clothes, a shower, and sleep with a blanket. I try to be less feral. I have to get up and out of this. Do some fucking yoga and get in contact with my inner self.

Motormouth Scotty

This is the time in my life where you may have noticed I've been hanging out with Scott the Motormouth all the time. When you're getting in deep, there is a tendency to want to find a partner to possibly throw your life away with, so it's less lonely. A junky duo of convenience, if you will. Maybe you think you can position your cocaine comrade as a pillow when you both land at the bottom of the bucket. Perhaps you feel less stupid if you can coax someone else into making the same stupid decisions as you. Intertwined dirtheads laughing each other on down the path of destruction, thinking their shallow loyalties will somehow come in handy.

Motormouth Scotty is a rich kid from the Bay Area. He has rebelled against his parents by being a Dead Head neo-hippy. Not so rebellious that he doesn't take their money, though. Instead of the spray-painted VW Bus, he has the Westphalia with the fancy pop-top sleeper in the roof, complete with a built-in stove and fridge. He shows up at Grateful Dead concerts with that baby loaded up with a tank of nitrous, ecstasy, mushrooms, weed, coke, all for sale or trade—pussy preferred.

He doesn't have the dreads, but he has long black hair that he uses $20 avocado conditioner on, and he keeps it tied back all tight and shiny. With his sharp nose, chin, high cheekbones, and ectomorphic soccer player build, he could be Native American Indian. Way too pale, though. He's a manicured, Svengali/trust fund hippy. The kid knows how to party.

Scotty fancies himself a Fox Mulder at an ayahuasca ceremony. The truth is closer to if Robert Downy Jr. had an ass baby with Ben Stiller in a Sedona sweat lodge that offered cucumber water at the end. He's handsome, I guess. And the hippy girls always come running to hear him spout his feminist mantras. He believes them, but he uses it so strategically to entice them, does it even count anymore? He spews pro-goddess platitudes between conspiracy theories and how-to guides on creating the best high utilizing certain drugs from Amazonian shaman recipes based on a book he heard about where the pages are made of bark and lettered in monkey blood. The author was known for binding his balls into tiny bark baskets, so you know it's legit!

I sometimes share Scott's couch with his white wolf, my friend, Luna. She knows I'm having a tough time. She'll come out from Scott's room halfway through the night and sleep against my feet to try and transfer some of her positive dog energy to me. It works.

Scott's birthday is exactly equidistant from mine, six months to the day, either direction. We were born on each other's half birthdays. Maybe we should have taken this as a *gypsy sign of ill omen* and just divided up the city.

I know Scott from Pot Plant Sarah back in the Isla Vista days, and now he's living at the Hitchcock House with Luna, Chapman, Satsi, Tina, and other partiers and musician types. It's a real compound. Sarah has a giant vegetable and sunflower garden out back in their substantial one-acre yard, and I don't even have to look in the middle to know there are probably some pot plants hidden in there. The view is protected from the street, and driving by you wouldn't even notice that it's there, next to the car dealerships. Perfect for the nefarious activities of a seditious party gang, just far enough away from downtown as to be a semi-restful oasis away from it all. We drink just as much but usually skip the cocaine there. Try to stick to weed Sunday-Wednesday.

I *have* made a few grand selling pounds to Scotty out there from Seattle Carl. He's friends with the Bolivian twins, Monica and Diana. Five years ago, these were the girls whose car I'd tried to siphon gas out of to make a bomb in a failed attempt at torching the police station because the cops had scabbed up the love of my life's face.

Carl has been driving down a shit ton of green bud from Washington every month stashed in the panels of his car. And Motormouth Scotty loves to buy primo green buds by the pound for the right price. Oh, he sure does! And right now, I have access to the best stuff for the best deal in the whole county. The problem is, neither of them will front because the buyer should never front. You never know what is going to be in that bag. They will say, "It's the *Chocolate Buddha Thai*," and it's really the motherfucking *Make you Want to Cry*.

Meanwhile, the value of money is constant and unarguable, so the buyer always has the pole position. If you're going to get weed or money fronted as the middleman, it has to be the weed. The buyer wants to see it, hold it, and smell it before fessing up the duckets. At that point, he can shit or get off the pot. But Carl doesn't know me for shit. He has been burned before he keeps saying. Much as I try to add extra talents and charms, he just won't budge. I can't get him to front me the weed.

I have to put the two parties together, which, as the middleman, is a potentially fucked situation. You risk having to argue over your cut later. They both start acting all confused, "Oh, I thought you were getting your cut on the other side. What did we talk about? Oh, now I don't remember."

This is a test in Scotty's and my *best friends forever* status, and he passes it. Scott does me right and shells out my dough without lagging on the payment. But that was only for a few transactions so far. A couple of thousand bucks to me. Not bad. All I want in this life right now is my own room somewhere with my own key to lock the door. I'm almost there. Going into my mid-twenties already and I've never had that. A room with a door that locks. You motherfuckers out there take that shit for granted.

Unfortunately, I arrive at Motormouth Scotty and Pot Plant Sarah's house a week later to see Seattle Carl driving out of the driveway. I guess they decided to cut out the middleman. I'm not stupid enough to expect perfect loyalty from a drug buddy, but shit, that's pretty harsh. I guess I shouldn't have been trying to make $200 per pound. I'm making money off coke and ecstasy so I can afford the loss, I guess.

Over my lifetime, this vice-based relationship with Motormouth Scotty will cost me much. Things like this are always disguised as fun activities in the beginning. We go up into the mountains shooting off the machine gun that he has to protect his large drug stash. It turns out we're both crack shots. We spell out people's names and snort them to prove our love. It all seems so jokey and ridiculous that we don't see what harm could come from it.

Ol' Motormouth Scotty does have some good qualities and possibly deserves a better name than this, but it's just too fun. I kind of talked up the more ridiculous aspects of his being, and I'm afraid I don't regret that. You guys don't want to hear about the days we were normal, right? I didn't think so.

I will say that Motormouth Scotty more than lives up to this name after midnight on Thursday, Friday, and Saturday once his nostrils are good and caked with blow. "Dude, we should go up to the Mission and dump blood on that Junipero Serra statue they put in! That piece of shit Indian killer! We actually allow a statue of him here? Blood! Real blood! We'll dump it all over his Indian killing hands!"

Weirdly, Pot Plant Sarah spots a problem with this. "Dude? Real blood? That would make us just as bad as the Indian killers. I don't know who this Junipero guy is, but I do know that an eye for an eye leaves the whole world blind."

I'm quick to respond. "Ok Sarah, Junipero Serra is the Spanish priest that enslaved the Native Americans and forced them to build all of the California Missions. And they have a statue of the piece of shit right out front of the Santa Barbara Mission! There are bones of his Chumash Indian slaves mixed into the foundation underneath that statue's feet!"

"Yeah, it ain't right," confirms Satsi.

"We should use tar and feathers. Someone drive out to the beach and get us some tar! We're going to feather this bitch up! Get a twelve-pack too. I'll pitch in later," lies Brandon Chapman. (Due to natural oil seepage in the Santa Barbara Channel, big globs of oily tar cover our beaches from time to time. It's pretty lame.)

I'm laughing my ass off in the corner, happy that Scott is stuck inside his brain thinking about the plan, unable to foist an extended verbal shit show upon us for a short moment.

Satsi, a longhaired dude that can beat me at Jeopardy, reviews the plan, "We'll tar and feather him, then dump on the blood, then piss on him, then cover him in lighter fluid, then light up his tar-balled head like a Roman candle."

"Yes!" Scott, Brandon, and I all say at once, shaking all of our heads, causing Brandon, Satsi, and Scott's ponytails to wag.

Pot Plant Sarah is out, "Well, you guys have fun going to jail. I'm pretty sure they frown on city landmark/church arson. I'm up for a good time, but I draw the line at church…arson. I'll be here drinking beer and smoking weed. You guys are too much of pussies anyway. You'll end up passed out in the rose garden, cold, out of beers, paint bucket spilled in the car. I know you stupid fuckers. You should invest in a clown car to arrive at these capers in."

"It's not even a church, Sarah. It's technically a mission," I say.

It's true, a massive sprawling mission overlooking the city, big grass yard out in front with a million rose bushes. That Junipero, he sure knew where the best spot was to build his *boogieman in the sky* houses. The Catholic Church probably sent him a boat full of choir boys for this one. Good real estate right there—these gold goblets aren't going to pay for themselves.

"Wait, I have another idea!" starts a newly energized Motormouth Scotty.

"Nooooo!" we all yell. Within minutes we are sucked into another line of bullshit and forget all about our plan.

Motormouth Scotty is usually fun, and chicks think they love his big booming deep voice until three in the morning. They realize, too late, he has no intention of shutting it up. If they are lucky, by four, he might be quiet long enough to slip his half-hard pud into them for a few seconds, before selfishly coming and falling asleep. At least then, they can rest that some type of *level* was completed. Otherwise, he will keep talking and talking and getting to no fucking point about anything, his brain firing off synapses in all directions, often forgetting what he's talking about mid-sentence and just starting a whole other monologue.

"The Freemasons are stealing babies for sacrifices and...and what was I?... Did you know China is coating our cookware with chemicals that make us angry and confused!? Teflon, man! Shit's diabolical. Alien technology fuckin' us up, bro! Congress is complicit. Half of them are aliens anyway, dude! The House Speaker is a fucking lizard, you guys!"

We all watch him, looking for the gills that he must be using not to have to take breaths as he continues to *ramperbant* us into oblivion. We try to get a word in edgewise, and he raises his jazz hands to signal that he may be getting to the point, for us to be patient, but he never fucking does! He does this until dawn at least once a week, and you can't escape it by trying to sleep in the next room with a pillow over your head. His big, booming voice passes between walls like Jackie Chan's foot through a piece of balsa wood. There will be no escape. Not at this address. I just need a room somewhere no one knows about that has a lock.

Sometimes Scotty, I, and whoever else is still up at dawn, will play frisbee golf on the Santa Barbara City College Campus, the most beautiful college campus in all the world. At seven in the morning, it's all ours.

At the most valuable corner of Santa Barbara's Mesa, a plateau rises about 50-feet to its perfectly manicured, 10-acre lawn. Looking off the top, it provides impressive views across the football field, running track, marina, Ledbetter Beach, the pier, and all down the coast. It is an endless view of palm trees, red-tiled roofs, and the expansive blue sea that is edged by the Channel Islands. Just beautiful. Crazy that a city college got this real estate and not an Ivy League university. Chalk one up for the kids that got all Cs.

We look insane, tossing our frisbees at seemingly nothing all over the campus. But there is a target. We just pick something like a park bench, a door that we know is around a corner or even just a tree, way off in the distance, and see who can hit it in the least number of throws. Sometimes, a teacher or someone who figures they are almost alone on the campus at 7 am, will go near one of our randomly assigned targets, and they will look over and become terrified when they suddenly see four guys all tossing sharp, hard frisbees at them.

One time, I shank hard left and hit some poor Japanese tourist who is there enjoying the morning peace. Poor bastard has no idea what's going on, and when I run towards him to explain, he runs away, all scared that he is in the middle of some abstract mugging scam for his expensive camera.

Frisbee golf is the only decent exercise I get since I moved downtown. Sometimes I do pullups and pushups at the little outdoor community gym by the bocce ball courts on amply treelined Anapamu Street. I don't really skate anymore because the cops are total dicks downtown and will ticket you for rolling your wheels on any type of pavement near State Street. I've stopped surfing too, unfortunately. I could use that Zen in my life right now.

We run after our Nasa developed plastic discs, and I climb up roofs and trees to get people's frisbees that get stuck. We take wind-sheltered breaks to smoke weed and chop lines of cocaine on the tops of the frisbees. And when the last of the coke wears off, we go eat breakfast at The Cajun Kitchen. I always get the Steve Special: scrambled eggs with cheddar cheese, beef and bean chili, sour cream on top with a big chunk of cornbread. After that 3,000-calorie bomb, it's time to crash long and deep, before going out to the bars and starting it all over. Cheers to being in your 20s, when a bender like this doesn't result in two days of nausea and a fear of the outside world so strong you flinch when the dog hops on the couch.

The Mad Cat Saga

A new bar has just opened, and nobody is controlling the cocaine sales in there yet. The Mad Cat is full of ultra-hip LA kids here to go to college. They'll need some coke, I figure. In the Mad Cat, there are red velvet circular couches, red vinyl booths, and red bar stools bolted to the ground up against the black bar. The walls are black as well, barely perceivable in the low lighting. Everything red and black. The colors of hell. Very apt.

Motormouth Scotty and I start hanging out there every night, and after a month, everybody adores us. We are charming, witty, well-groomed, and we have coke and weed. If there is a line to get in, we just go right in the front as the bouncer waves us through. Maybe we'll pick a lucky girl out of the crowd to come in with us. We don't have to even pay for drinks.

I arrange for a large Mexican, who I know from the juvenile hall days, to accompany me for the first few nights until rookies get the clue. Locals only. If you're from LA, you have to pay. These rich LA kids come up here with their giant bags of weed, coke, and ecstasy. They think they can start selling wherever and to whomever they want. "Nuh, uh, buddy.

Not in this bar. You see that big guy over there? This is his gang's territory. You really don't want to get seen selling in here again."

"Oh, I'm sorry, man, that's crazy. I didn't know about things being all divvied up like that, bro." They always say some shit like that.

Daniel hasn't joined a gang, he just works out too much and wears a Raiders hat. But that type of talk scares LA kids, so fuck it. It's free sailing after that. Location isn't always everything, sometimes it's timing as well. I was set. I can't bring enough bindles in. These fuckin' LA college kids used to party with Drew Barrymore and shit, so their nostrils are like Hoover vacuums, distended and gory by the end of the night. I'm scared of the amount that I am suddenly required to bring in. I'm stashing all these separate bags of coke in my fuckin' underwear. I'm still on felony probation. So, what am I going to do? Start dragging ounces of it around?

The manager of the bar, the biggest coke head in there, says, "J.C., if you can't bring enough in each night, we'll have to get someone else to relieve you when you run out, which is what, by midnight?"

"Actually, that sounds fine. Tell the second shift to never come a minute earlier than midnight, and to be honest, they will probably make plenty. I get nervous after midnight, and I like to be done by then. Every time some really heinous, *railer-bucket* shit goes down, it's after midnight." I guess I do work here, kind of. Sure, we'll let the nosy manager make the call. She's right anyway.

I do not feel comfortable trying to keep up with the growing hunger for white dope in this joint. I'm spooked as fuck, to be honest. What am I doing? I have a 2-year, suspended prison sentence. If I get caught selling coke while on probation for selling weed, it's easy to see that I am on an upward progression in my criminal career. The judges in Santa Barbara toss out prison sentences like it's nothing. Don't let the California beach town vibe relax you too much. We, as a single state in the union, put more people in prison than Russia. If I were to be caught with all this shit individually bagged for a quick sale? Yeah, I'd be going to the state penitentiary. Let me also reiterate that I'd be considered "pretty" in prison.

The party strip in Santa Barbara is one mile long down State Street. Mel's Bar is the eye of the stretched-out oval of the liver disease hurricane. Little bars and restaurants shoot down the side streets for a block on each side of State Street. Little roads that are named after the Spanish families that were mostly chased out by the next batch of colonizers 200 years ago.

I always go to the same few bars, so people don't have to look too hard for me. If my probation officer just used one of her Friday nights to check out every single bar in this one little blast zone of criminality, she would quickly find me. I would be standing here, close to the bathroom I call an office, all clammy lipped, talking up a storm to someone who isn't even listening. They are just waiting for me to pause for a millisecond so they can jump in and get a jawgasm, excitedly about absolutely anything that pops into their dope scrambled brain.

I really believe something about jaw movement releases dopamine for these people. You could chop deep-sea cable in little Daphne's mouth right now. Even when they don't have someone immediately to blast with multiple word salads, you can still see that jaw, gyrating, and clamping down, creating a layer of wet enamel dust between their molars.

My probation officer would probably handcuff me right here, before walking me straight into the bathroom for a cavity search. My only plan for this situation is that she won't want to search inside my underwear. For reals, gangster? Ha! That's probably the first place she's going to dig. Get a real good cup on my nuts, make some eye contact, swish around for the little thin dress sock that contains all the separate cocaine bindles in there. "Oh, what have we here, Mr. Scales? Is it three years in the pen plus two added years that were suspended from the last time you fucked up? Oh, I believe it is." Then she'd smear the sock on my face, getting my own nut sweat on my lips, laughing maniacally. Brutal.

These are the intrusive scenarios that I ruminate on as I toss and turn on some stranger's couch that I had to promise I was holding onto a final bindle for them before they would agree to let me crash for the night. Why in the fuck am I doing this? The money. Pure and simple. Everybody does it for the same reasons. Throws their life away. Money. Some idiots do it for a piece of sociopathic ass, but that ain't me. I only let these crazy chicks wind me up so much. When it gets weird, I just hang out in a new bar for a few nights, maybe go down to Elsie's; they'll never look in there. Wait until her mom tracks her down and starts making her go to Alcoholics Anonymous meetings again.

The reason I'm doing it is that I need to get enough money to get a place to live. With first, last, and deposit? That'd be $2,000. But I always snort too much and give too much away at the after parties with friends. I never even get up to a $1,000 somehow.

Things are going all right in the beginning. Girls who never would have paid attention to me before, now whisper, with obviousness to their girlfriends that they want to get in my pants. I just don't know that by "pants," they mean the pocket where the coke is. I have a smile on my face, gel in my hair, and a mental penis the size of a watermelon. I'm the King of the Mad Cat.

I feel like this is the only way I can make a living, and I have to be able to justify that it isn't idiotic, so I tell myself whatever I want to hear. And in this town, it probably is one of the only ways I can live. With my reputation for telling people what I think about them and my theoretical resume, even if it materialized, would get me about $8.50 an hour in a town that costs $700 a month just for a room. Let's see, after taxes, I would have to borrow money *and* eat ramen every meal just to make rent. The way I see it, this is it. And I'm fucking doing it. Take me to prison! Better than working at Mickey D's!

At least this is my position at this time. Which apparently, after looking it up, is the position that possibly comes right before the one where you grab your ankles in prison. But for now, I'm having a ball! I am a natural drug salesman. I could sell a sense of shame to a politician.

One night, the doorman sends me a messenger from the front. "Hey, there's some undercovers in here. Cool it off."

For some reason, cops will announce themselves to the doorman because they think that since he's in the security business, he wants to be a cop someday. By the time the police make it to the back, I was warned ten minutes ago, and I'm out the back door. Off to snort the rest of the bindles, which start off being one or two a night, then more and more.

A bindle is a piece of paper—ripped up pornography is my personal sales gimmick—folded origami-style for the purpose of holding a little less than a half-gram of low-grade coke cut with caffeine powder. When you do your last line at 5 am, you can use my *pornigami* to jack off with, all by yourself, cold sweat reservoir on your upper lip, as you clutch with your free hand the edge of the sink, trying not to look at your clammy face in the bathroom mirror. In finality, you desperately lick the paper as you start to bust, trying to get the last of the crappy white powder into your system as a humiliating jizz duet to your sad cum load. The disgrace that sets in after that is monumental. Time to toss and turn in your cold-sweated shame-bed for the two hours until dawn. It's only Friday! Only two more nights to go!

You think you won't come back to the bar again tonight, but you will. And when you see me, you will look away. Pretend you were hoping I wouldn't be here. But we both know that's just a lie that your subconscious mind was telling your conscious mind to get you here. You're embarrassed, and a little surprised at how quickly the cocaine fangs come out once the sun goes down. You hesitate, but once you've got a little bit of courage up from Dr. Tanqueray and Soda, you turn from the bar and panic when you can't quickly track me down with your eyes. I see the relief on your face when you finally find me. I laugh on the inside. You're a regular. Don't fight it, bitch.

This is the only time in my life I have ever felt like what you would call a piece of shit. I justify it because, in my mind, its mostly LA douche bags invading my town that I'm selling to. The little fuckers that act all smug because they know their parent's money will always be there to catch them if they fall. I, myself, think I'm pretty cool there for a while until I have to do some authentic soul searching. That's a lot of parties away, however.

One night after we close down the bar, everybody meets at Tyler and Motormouth Scotty's new pad for a weed, coke, and Ween party. Ween is a phenomenal band that is the only other thing besides the crowd's adoration at the Mad Cat that matters to Scotty and me. Soon, we have the God-Ween-Satan album blasting, and I say, "Ok Scotty, roll some video. Hello, people of earth. What I intend to do is take this huge bong hit and snort this foot-long line of coke, simultaneously!"

Scott has his video camera ready to roll, and I have the giant line of coke ready to snort and the bong ready to hit.

Ignition. *Snooo-bublbub-shrnnnrrrrrt-blublub-snrrrt-bubablrbluh-sloooorrrrrrt.*

Things go beautifully until I reach the end of the line of coke, and my nose starts gushing blood. I spit out a giant cloud in a panicked explosion of pot smoke. Blood drops enter the intense hurricane from my upper lip, and they become instant aerosol, giving the cloud's top edge a pinkish hue. They are part of the contact high now. Perhaps the audience will receive some of my Highlanderesque essences. Oh, shit. Here comes the coke into my brain. LOOOOOOPY DOO-DAH!!!!!!!

A week or so before, Motormouth Scotty had punched out a guy in the Mad Cat for me because it was my final warning to not cause any more trouble in there, or the 86-classification was going to be permanent this time. The head bouncer, as far as I can tell, is serious, and he should be given a cushy pension for how patient he has been with me. The bouncers take our side, we were obviously trying to behave better by me not being the one to punch the guy, and they just tell us to leave for the night. It's early, and we don't know what to do with ourselves.

We go to a guy named Zak's house and buy 20 hits of ecstasy out of his architect blueprint storage tube for $12 a pop. Pure shit. We go to Scotty's other friend's house and sit in her jacuzzi, high as fuck. Motormouth Scotty goes to fuck the girl, and I'm just sitting in there for hours.

Scott comes back, and we do some more X. I jokingly hold up the bag of about a dozen capsules and say, "Let's not do all of this tonight." Well, we didn't, you'll be happy to know. It will actually take us until halfway into tomorrow. When I get out of that jacuzzi after four hours, I'm wrinklier than Bob Dole's balls.

Scotty says he is fine to drive, so we are off to the next adventure. We get pulled over because he's driving 15 mph in a 30 zone. The cops ask Motormouth why one of his eyes is bouncing up and down. I'm already planning ways to get out of prison sex when Scotty just straightens up, instantly sober, and comes up with this bullshit story about how it's an eye condition called *reticular-spenditis*. The cops let us go. Apparently, all the drugs and alcohol we are on cancel each other out, and our pupils—one of them bouncing no less—must have been the proper size. Motormouth avoids a field sobriety test, and he is a little pissed about that because he says he was ready to pass that shit. Scotty needs to settle the fuck down and see a significant victory for what it is.

Ween, *The Mollusk* Tour

How does one begin to describe Ween? Two brothers, not related, playing music to and with each other since they were kids in a small Pennsylvania town across the Delaware River from New Jersey. George Washington stayed there before his famous crossing of the Delaware. Not much has happened there since. Until now.

After more than a decade of playing together, Mickey and Aaron have now become Dean and Gene Ween. They've created a band with such an incredible knowledge of how music works technically and in such an expansive way, that they can genre leap from masterpiece to masterpiece with a complete lack of care for transition. This results in a series of cold-water splashes of severe contrast that invigorates the crowd more and more as they wonder what might come next.

The crowd looks up, open-mouthed, and in awe of the classic mastery that transpires one moment to the next. Ween will start with a *burlesque ditty* of absurdist art then dive right into a song that sounds like Prince, but somehow better than Prince. Van Halen, but better than Van Halen! It's unbelievable. One day aliens will find Ween CDs in our rubble and say,

"This! This must have been the most popular band of their time. This frarking glorbs!!"

Ween is ALL of the categories. They jaggedly rip between jam bandy to Psilocybin punk, skewering showbiz narcissism, creating an improved version of it made of parody and satire. All this interspersed with down to earth, hilarious, sometimes X-rated between-song banter that even a seasoned *blue comic* would enjoy. Ween is the anti-prima donna.

Critically hated and forever underrated. Rolling Stone magazine gave this magnum opus of an album, *The Mollusk*, that they are currently touring on, only three and a half stars. In the same season, they give the band Smashmouth the number three album of the entire fucking year. Three and a half stars for the most underrated album of the late 1990s. *Rolling Stone* magazine shall henceforth be referred to as "Trash Rag."

To make the recording, Dean and Gene obscured themselves at the tip of an island in New Jersey after all the summer vacationers had left. They were truly alone to finish the critical work of inventing the music for this epic series of ocean tunes. There were no distractions, absolutely nothing else to do but walk the beach and throw heavy fish lines out into the grey surf when their brains were pushed past the limit of unparalleled and unique creativity. By mid-winter, the pipes froze and burst, and they return home one day to find all of their musical equipment half submerged. But the tapes were saved! Up there! On the table. Thank Poseidon!

It's time to pack it up and finish the album somewhere else. Enough of the lonely essence of the sea had been captured on the tapes, shaping the record, germinated and cultivated by the dark looming surf and the solitude of the grey beach. The theme had materialized. The pirate songs were good!

Only Jimi Hendrix himself is better than Dean Ween on the *gee-tar*, and Gene Ween can whisper the sweetest lullabies or wail until all the town's dogs are barking. A lot of their earlier music was a bit discordant and insane, so I can see why some people see them as 'niche.' But with this new album, there are so many brilliant, melodic moments. It's basically a series of psychedelic sea shanties, yet I feel like you could play it to a rest home or a kindergarten, a sorority house, or a biker bar, and people would dig it.

I want them to receive their well-deserved commercial success, but a selfish part of me wants to keep seeing them in 1,000 people or fewer capacity theatres, not blown out mega venues. *The Mollusk* is the album that should push them over the edge, which makes me a little sad. I greedily want to keep having them mostly to myself, sharing them with only a global family of about a million brilliant weirdos and a few idiots.

Tonight, join Dean, Gene, Dave, Claude, and Glenn as they—for 34 songs!—become nautical acid pirates for your utter glee, showcasing their new record, *The Mollusk!*

Josh Keppel and I drive to the LA show. Alex and Motormouth Scotty go to the San Francisco show the night prior. SF or LA is a choice Santa Barbarians often have to make when bands skip us over on their way up the California coast. Alex and Motormouth sure blew it, and I'm glad about it. Had they been here, my night would possibly not have happened the same way. That would have been a tragedy. This is about to be the greatest show I have attended since Jane's Addiction's *Nothing's Shocking* tour I went to a decade ago. Buckle up, Buttercups! Shit's about to get wild as fuck!

We find parking down a side street in the mid-Wilshire area of LA that is known as Miracle Mile. Tonight *will* be miraculous, so it's apt as fuck! We make our way to the El Rey Theatre, capacity less than 800. Perfect! Built-in the 1930s in the popular Art Deco style that was reminiscent of the time, the El Rey is a high class, single-screen movie theatre with a big bright marquee that has those four magic letters on it. WEEN.

As we walk up, I can imagine Lauren Bacall stepping out of a Rolls Royce in a long silk dress for her newest movie premiere, long cigarette holder dangling in her gloved fingers as she steps out onto the red carpet. Humphrey Bogart himself is getting out behind her, himself half trashed on whiskey already.

We get inside, and there is a gigantic, lit up crystal chandelier hanging from the high ceiling, threatening to kill us all if there's an earthquake. Or if Dean goes in too hard on a monster solo. You can feel the excitement percolating out of the drug-soaked super fans that are so dedicated to this band that if you called them a cult, you could make a debate team stutter trying to say otherwise. Their wild eyes tell the whole story; this is the end of their pilgrimage to Mecca. A live Ween show.

This album, as well as being the most accessible, will also be the band's most fabulous. Ween knows it too, and it shows in the performance. They're having the times of their lives up there, playing barefooted, drinking from a 5th of Jack Daniels—as they are known to do at each show. Look at them. Beautiful.

The show opens with "I'll be Dancing in the Show Tonight," a burlesque-ditty with a touch of the Monty Python. Smoke envelopes Dean and Gene until only their silhouettes are visible, surrounded by the neon glow of pink, green and blue lights. Then, masterpiece after masterpiece just rolls out.

"The Golden Eel" mesmerizes us in a deep, dark, underwater fantasy waltz. The eel is brought to life by the bubbling, low-pitched modular synths. The light show at play here as it interacts with the profuse amount of machine created fog adds to the effect. Mushrooms would actually be too much. This IS the mushrooms. Oh wait, I *did* take mushrooms. Oh shit, there they are. *Wheeeee!*

They jump into, "Baby Bitch," my personal favorite, and all the chicks in the room go nuts. They consider for a moment throwing their underwear at Dean, then realize they aren't wearing any. They have fallen prey to a bittersweet, vengeful, yet triumphant love song. "Baby Bitch" is dreamy and enchanting, with the amount of self-deprecating anger and humor that makes you see it in your own past. Elliot Smith, four years gone already, should have stayed alive to see this. He might have laid the dagger down.

"The Mollusk," the album's eponymous song comes on. It would be like "Octopus's Garden," if The Beatles were prog rock. The fluttery flute lures us deep down into the grotto of sound. Everyone is in the groove now, and it is clear we are about to see a legendary display of ability and magic of an impressive duration—the band has already told us so themselves—we are rapt and ready, lulled by a goodnight song for the shellfish. Then the flutes take off down the currents, and we are soon passing up the tunas, continually swept along by a delightful sonic undertow.

Soon, the crowd is singing along to the classic, "Buenas Tardes Amigo." Magnificent. A strumming acoustic guitar weaves an epic tale of murder, revenge, and secrecy whose intensity unfolds throughout the song like a cathedral of sound. Its story concerns a wandering Mariachi who finds a campfire in the desert. Sitting at the campfire is his target, who, vendetta not yet known to him, is willing to trade a bowl of chicken and beans for a song. Little does he know in the beginning that the song is about **him.** *"You, you keeled my brotherrrrr…last weeenter. You shot HIM! Two times…in the backkkk!"*

The generous stranger starts figuring out that something is amiss, but he realizes too late. His throat seizes. *Poison!*

The mariachi continues his song to the "alleged" murderer of his brother. As he wriggles on the ground in pain, the mariachi bends over him for a closer look, as the foam from his mouth drips down onto the scorpion infested sand. The wolves howl, sensing something is about to die. In a surprise twist, the Mariachi says, *"It was I, who killed him…and now the truth, I'll never…have… to say."*

It's incredible to hear hundreds of people at once scream, *"Perhaps…. I'd sellllll you a cheeeckin'…wit poison, interlaced wit zee meat!"* We are all psychically connected in a chorus, ready for wide-scale revolt or an orgy. Beware the deranged Mariachi!

"Buckingham Green," is a roller coaster of childlike wonder contrasted with mysterious, majestic orchestral instrumentation. The solemn and beautiful aspects of Gene's voice are truly showcased here. You just want to kiss his forehead as you watch him almost shed a tear over the child on Buckingham Green, who is kept very clean. The song slowly builds to a torrential but short guitar clinic by Dean, before he hands it back to Glenn, the keyboardist for a romp of his own.

The band suddenly leaves the stage after playing for two hours. But we aren't ready. We scream and beg for an encore. We get it. We knew we would. I'm screaming, "Weeeeeeen!!!" They start with, "Dr. Rock," a roller coaster off the tracks! Pure rock and roll. Our eardrums are taking a beating and loving it like George Bush Sr. when Barbara puts on the leather. "Dr. Rock," is like a Kiss song if Kiss was good. The light show and the smoke machine are working overtime. Suddenly, they scream, "BREAK! " while down-stroking savage power cords at peak volume. The resulting contrast of the quietness as we stand there in awe is almost as moving as the loudness was.

We roar our approval!

"Blarney Stone" is a chance for Dean to take a break from just endlessly shredding the guitar. A lewd, rude Irish sea shanty propped up by an accordion. You can almost see the salt water splashing on the decks, and you can smell Black Beard's breath as he belts out the tune, resistant wench in the arm that doesn't end in a hook.

For "Ocean Man," Gene pulls out this funky little mandolin and plays the fuck out of it in a fizzy trop-rock number. Deaner goes on his third or fourth exquisite guitar solo. Awesome, giddy fun. I am yelling the songs I want them to play that they haven't done yet. "Mutilated Lips!" "Let me lick your Pussy!"

"Tears for Eddie," you can almost see the tears falling off Deaner's guitar strings. Sometimes the sad things are the happiest things. Through his closed eyelids, you can sense his eyeballs rolling up into a different dimension where everybody gets to see their dead dog again. Maybe Eddie isn't a dog for everybody. But to me, when I listen to this song, Eddie is a beloved family dog that saved the whole family from a house fire, only to be killed by the smoke after going back in for the turtle.

"Captain Fantasy," pure, unadulterated rock and roll. I don't know who

Captain Fantasy is, but he will always be one of my favorite superheroes. Wolverine can shine your shoes, man. The whole band just pounds away for this one, and it's a big happy family up there. Claude is about to beat through his drum.

"Wouldn't you like to be?! Somewhere floating free?! Captain Fantasy!!" Gene let's out in a helium shriek. Oh, but I am, Gener. I **am** floating free!

Then, a short reprise of the show's opening song; a quick, out of place bookend to the concert, "Dancing in the Show Tonight." And then it's over for real.

We just all stand there, used up, and flapping emptily in the breeze. No longer able to understand the world that waits outside for us, having just been transported several galaxies away, we slowly remember how to speak English and start to shuffle off towards the doors...amazed... different. Our brains are reeling from the orgasmic audio buffet we just gorged on. A sprawling universe of different sounds and feelings. Two and a half hours of riding a sonic carpet into an exotic and multi-dimensional world fraught with pleasures and adventure not thought possible before: a live Ween show.

This concert I will add to my trifecta of amazing shows which triangulate my transition to manhood:

First, there was Jane's Addiction, on the *Nothing's Shocking* tour; balls reach fruition.

Second? Ozzy getting on stage with Black Sabbath for the first time in 20 years; balls begin wearing a cape, sipping cognac, and tapping out melodies on cobblestones with the tips of their ivory handled canes.

And now this, Ween, on *The Mollusk* tour; balls wear a monk robe, and their eyes spin in their sockets like blindingly bright, tiny whirlpool galaxies.

The amulet triptych is complete; I have reached enlightenment. I could turn into a glowing fog of stardust and float onto the moon right now, and I wouldn't be surprised.

Wait, where did Josh go? Did he weasel backstage? I lost track of him in all the bliss. There are hundreds of people milling around confusedly, and I can barely find the tips of my shoes myself, much less Josh. I think he may have gotten a pass from a photographer that had gotten enough shots early and bounced. Josh is a news station cameraman familiar with the ins and outs of press passes. Did Josh ditch me? There was only one pass, so of course, he did. Meanwhile, I'm supposed to wait out here without even an apparent bar to drink in and wait? This is bullshit. Touché, Josh. Fuckin' touché.

But then...something amazing happens. I hear these toughened LA security guards say, "Ok, we'll let the kid meet Ween."

I'm literally right there, so I'm like, *Who's meeting Ween? I'm* meeting Ween! And I look to my left, and I see that this mentally disabled kid has made Ween a big chocolate chip cookie face and big wavy red licorice hair in the shape of their mascot, the Boognish. Totally awesome.

The kid is fucking adorable, too. I can see how these hardened tough guy's hearts have been melted. And then, I see a split-second opportunity. The kid and his friends are a bit slow to react. I instantly sober up and snake the chance they hadn't yet realized was there, "All right, Johnny, let's go. We're going to go meet Ween." I say.

Security thinks I'm his helper, and his friends think I'm the theater manager or something. Next thing you know, Cookie Boy and I are being walked up the steps, across the stage, up some little ladder stairs, and Gene Ween answers the door. He takes one look at the kid and the Boognish cookie and says, "Come on in guys, welcome to the party!"

Are you fuckin' crazy?! I get in, and Dean Ween is sitting on some carpet with his girlfriend and about a dozen other people. The room is bubbling with big smiles all around. "What a show! You guys killed it," I gush.

Guess who's in there with a cold bottle of beer in his hand already? Motherfucking Josh Keppel. His eyes get all big, and then he starts smiling and saying he was going to try to come out and get me. Ha-ha. Yeah, right, Josh. It's ok, baby. When it comes to getting backstage, it's every man for himself. I once left a scorching hot girl out front of the venue to get backstage at Alice in Chains. Not only was she gone when I got out, but I heard she left with some dude I hated to make a point. Don't sweat it, Josh. I don't even have titties.

Soon, I'm in the after-party groove, I'm barefoot like their trademark schtick, and I'm drinking out of the same Jack Daniel's bottle they had cracked open on stage, eating all their broccoli and ranch dressing. The disabled kid has been gone for a while, and I see the manager whispering to Gene. I imagine something along the lines of "Um, were we responsible for keeping the handicapped kids together?"

I figure I better make a friend quick, so I go over to Dean and say, "Hey Deano, great show, man. You like to party?" I rub the side of my nose a little bit, in an obvious hint that I'm talking about a *powder party*.

"It's not speed, is it?" Dean replies.

"Hell no, it's the *Peruvian marching flake!*" I say reassuringly.

This is a lie. It's the Tijuana Baby Laxative. But you guys, please forgive me. I had to be able to tell Motormouth I did blow with Dean Ween!

Next thing you know, Dean, his girlfriend, and I are in a tiny bathroom doing blow off the back of the toilet. Dean is smiling at me and patting me on the shoulder as I tell him the story of how I got in there. He's a little creeped out at first, but after seeing the big pile of blow I'm chopping up, he's soon laughing his ass off.

"A bit stalkery, but a stalker with blow is a stalker I can know," Dean declares.

The next day, we go to Venice Beach and meet Dean. Josh busts out his fancy camera, and we do an impromptu photoshoot amongst all the usual Venice Beach insanity. A street performer on roller skates cruises by, playing an electric guitar with a speaker built into itself. Josh flags this guy down, and soon we're listening to Dean play this crude thing out on the sidewalk, and people are stopping to take a look at the master.

"Should I put out a beanie? " Dean says, laughing.

I get a picture of Dean with his arm around my shoulders in a like *Hey, this dude is funny, I like him,* sort of way, not a *Hey, this guy stalked his way into my dressing room last night pretending to be a retarded kid's helper,* type of way.

Josh is excited to develop the pictures because he is as big of a Ween freak as me. Within a few days, I have my 8x10 glossies of Dean and me. What a memento to have for such an epic experience. Scotty and Alex don't believe me when I tell them the story. They *need* to not believe it because they went to the other show up north in San Francisco. Plus, it sounds so outrageous, even for me. Checkmate, motherfuckers! I whip out that glossy of Deano and me in Venice Beach, and they shit themselves. That shuts them right the fuck up.

I understand this story exudes a bit more hero worship than I usually like to exhibit. I mean, I'm almost immune to it. Steve McQueen? He didn't seem all that cool to me, get off his jock. Jimmy Page? That bitch stole all that shit from the Delta Blues musicians and never credited them. Plus, he likes his girls barely pubescent. Jimmy Carter? Ok, now there's a hero.

This should tell you how hardcore Ween fans are. Me, a guy who doesn't really even believe in heroes, would chew up and swallow a ghost pepper if Dean told me to do it. Then I would dry heave and cry. I'd cry because Dean Ween felt me worthy of entertaining him with my jackassery, if even for a fleeting moment.

Dean Ween is one of the most underrated gods of the guitar that have ever graced the planet. His playing just takes people to a place. It makes me feel invincible, happy, and worry-free. You've got to give the man his due. Thanks for the experience Deano! I'll see you on tour. I'll try to be a little less molesty next time. I definitely won't flash my middle-aged man tits to your tour bus 20 years from now.

Raisin Brain

Nursing whiskey-cocaine hangovers in the day, sitting in the bar at night. That's what I've been doing for a while now. Cocaine was never my thing. I used to shame people for it when they clogged up the bathrooms. Now, look at me. I actually *do* have morals, but the money keeps me in it.

I go to the bathroom at the Mad Cat one elegant evening to find that the door has been chain-sawed into a western-style saloon door dealio. You can see over the top if you're like 7-feet tall. I say, "What's the point of this?" Then I meet the new bouncer. Guess how tall he is? I guess the owner was bound to find out what type of bar he owns.

Luckily, this new bouncer loves weed. Can't get enough of it. Cool guy, actually. After developing some quick rapport with him, we come to an understanding. I gesture to him if a guy I don't like or know seems to be in the bathroom doing bumps or selling. Your clue is usually more than one person going in at once, one of them wearing a backwards Dodger hat. Wilt Chamberlain Jr. here will just saunter over and poke his head through the top of the door and yell at them, hopefully making them spill their bindles on the floor. He has to make a quota, and I need mostly exclusive rights to this bar. So, we work out a situation where everybody wins. *Boom-boom-a-bodda, I think I'll have a pina colada!* Basically, I just have to give him some pot at the beginning of the weekend.

A 6-foot blond girl named Rita shows up early at the Mad Cat one happy hour. Our friend Alex likes her but she doesn't say anything about him, and the next thing you know we are in the bathroom doing coke, and she's peeing in front of me.

Alex is a non-descript rich kid that you'd forget what he looks like two minutes after you met him. Absolutely nothing stands out or is interesting about him; a blank slate until Jeopardy comes on T.V. That's when he cleans house. Even on Tournament of Champions week. I guess you can say he's a nerdy, surfery, Rain Man. He's got straw-colored hair parted too far to the side and won't make eye contact when he talks to you. He focuses on the wall to the left behind your head, squinting at the Herculean effort that verbal communication is to him. He has a car and will drive anywhere at the drop of a hat. You just have to tell him there's going to be girls there for him to be afraid to talk to.

Also, we go to bars where I don't get free drinks sometimes. Alex might as well grab me a drink while he's up there getting his, right? That's half of why we keep him around, otherwise, he'd just sit in his room by himself all the time, watching documentaries, doing math puzzles, and masturbating to the same Playboy. The issue with fuckin' Nancy Sinatra in it—he's very attached to it. When you look at it in the corner of his room, you can just see the crust on the edges. You'd think surfer Rain Man would keep a tidy room, but there's nothing but dirty laundry, pizza boxes, college textbooks, something he's calling a "supercomputer" that he built. Also, a pitiful mattress on the ground up against the windows that have sheets thumbtacked over them. He can afford a way better room, but this is how he chooses to live. I hate it because I have to crash here sometimes.

In ten years, he will be worth a few million dollars from his job thwarting hackers for the government. For now, he's a disappointment to his father. You may think this is mean of us to use him for rides and drinks, but trust me, it's at least a fair trade. You try hanging out with a guy who develops an instant crush on any girl who smiles at him, and now he won't shut up about it all night afterwards. The fact he's aware and willingly accepts his lot is proof if you ask me. What's the term? Symbiotic? Yeah, we have a symbiotic relationship.

As if that's not enough, his main object of desire, his reason for living, is now here pulling down her pants in front of me to pee. Get this, her name is Rita B Good. I shit you not. With perfect apple titties like that? Wishful thinking when you named her that, pops. Girls will always pee in front of me. I mean, we are in a bathroom. Maybe they think I'll give them a more prominent line if they expose their little *fuzzy-tinkler* in my presence on the pretext of peeing.

So, Rita and I end up getting pretty wild later that night. Out of guilt, I tell Motormouth Scotty what I did, and he tells Alex, out of being an asshole. Now we're fighting, and the empire starts to crumble. Rita loves every minute of it. I see Scotty and Alex talking on the corner of State and Haley, near the bar we had been occupying opposite sides of. With revenge in my heart, I sneak up behind Motormouth Scotty and pull his legs out from under him. *Smack!!* His head hits the red tile of State Street. It's a horrible sound, and I feel instantly terrible, but they won't stay for my apology.

It will take weeks to get them back. They start bringing the Mad Cat against me, perhaps rightfully so. I'm going off the edge. I'm walking everywhere now too. I say to Alex, as close to sorry, without actually *being* sorry, "Alex. You were <u>never</u> going to get that chick by yourself. I was going to get her on *our team*, and transfer her to you, mostly undegraded."

"You think I can love her now after she was sordid with you? " he'd unforgivedly bleat. "I know what you guys did. I know how good you can be making nice girls bad, J.C. "

"Sorted? " I say, confused.

"Sor<u>d</u>id. " Says, Alex.

"Sworded? " I say, confident I'm getting closer.

"Sor<u>d</u>-debaucherous. Debaucherous, ok, J.C. "

"Just because her name is Rita <u>B Good</u> does NOT make it so, Alex. She came at me. I barely got her shirt off. She's still pristine. She only *looked* at my penis, she didn't *touch* it, all right? Maybe she *is* good. "

"No!" Alex is immovable, "She won't ever look the same to me again."

This fuckin' guy is like, from an Emily Bronte book or somethin'. I give up and let him settle down for a few weeks. Meanwhile, my shoes are wearing out from all the walking I have to do now that he won't let me in his car.

I start not being able to handle my liquor again and get my Jack and Cokes cut off. I accuse the bartender of taking their side and get kicked out entirely. I'm not even allowed in the Mad Cat for half of *the Mad Cat year*. It was only a matter of time before they figured it out, that I used to be a homeless skate rat selling dirt weed from a fanny pack.

It blows over all too quickly, though. Everybody loves me again soon enough, and I would do anything to keep that going. I don't know why, but the stardom that I have for the first time at the Mad Cat matters to me. Before, I'd always loved my notorious polarization of the crowd. But how quickly I'd fallen into the role of the bar's "Prom King." No one here knows that I used to live in a teepee or that I've been in a group home. I'm an imposter who just zipped off his old skin like a lizard, and now I'm playing a character without all the baggage. Just born and barely scarred. In the beginning, I could have named myself Vin and put on an Austrian accent. Oh, well.

I think it's me they like. I make people wait while I tell them a story before I give them their coke on the pretext that I have to wait until the coast is clear. But really, I just like telling stories to people. I always have. I think I feel lonely in this part of my life. Yeah, I'm really lonely. I'm reaching out for real contact, and all they can think is, *When is this asshole gonna shut up and reach into his sweaty ball bag and give me my shit?*

At least my stories are entertaining. I just listened to Montecito Monica tell the story about her fake suicide attempt when she didn't get a Maserati on her sweet 16. "Oh, you bet that bitch brought back the Benz 300 E. Then I totaled a Maserati the first month and told her it was because it was 'too yellow.' I wanted it to be Sedona Sunrise, Mom! Can you believe what a bitch I am, I mean, *was*?"

Fuck it, if this chick is telling cutter stories, I'm telling the one about the first time I busted a nut. Alex is already looking at her like she's wifey material. He's ready to drop to one knee. Fuck it, I'm goin' in, "So, there I was. Listening to a Blondie album, rocking back and forth, belly down on the family couch to Heart of Glass," I begin, to my audience of four or so.

"I'm just staring down at the album cover rocking back and forth, back and forth. I'm 14 and have just spotted my first little translucent nut-hair. It was like a microscopic jellyfish tentacle. Something starts stirring in my pants. I start staring *into* the album cover, deep into Blondie's eyes with a frenzied concentration, into her soul. She's telling me to *Be a man and come and get what I have to have.* I feel a strange tickling begin at the tip of my hardened purple mushroom cap as it reaches a hot enough friction against my jeans to raise a loaf of bread."

*Oh fuck. Why won't he give me the coke? I'll listen to anything **after** that. My* enslaved audiences are probably thinking while squirming for their fixes.

"*All right, Debbie. I'm comin' to ya'! Here it comes…tsssrrrrrrrrt. Ooooooohhhhh shit!* Something explodes in my pants! It's all soaked down there! Did I cut my dick on my zipper? I couldn't have. I'm wearing the 501 button flies. They're slice proof in the driest of humps. Thanks, Mr. Strauss! I look inside, and it turns out to be what looks like half a can of corn water. I haven't cut my dick on my zipper at all. I've become a man!!"

Fuck. What is this shit? Their suffering should be visible to me by now. Maybe I don't give a shit. I start wrapping it up before they leave and try their luck at O'Malley's.

"I still love you, Debbie Harry. If you ever want to tangle in the sheets, just say when and where. I love you. It's ok if you're fat or if you have gingivitis. When it comes to you and me, it will always be 1987. That day on the couch. I know you felt me staring into that album cover. You looked back into me, didn't you, Debbie? For the record, I am *not* stalking Debbie Harry. She knows where I am. She'll come eventually."

I slowly close my fist in front of my face in closure.

Finally! They rejoice.

These people fuckin' love my stories in here. I mistakenly think, the cocaine lying to me. Look, there's a new crop of people arriving. They're here for me. I know it's not the cocaine quality.

"Hey, did I ever tell you about the time I smashed a cop car windshield in a riot?" I say as they arrive up to me.

Hey man, we just want the blow, they're slumped shoulders seem to say.

Lynn Strait

It's now the end of 1998, and we are about to head into the last year before the *technology century* begins and turns us into a nation of open-mouthed screen-starers. The year a Prince album was named for. It's December, and some of my crash spots have been falling through. I've been stuck sleeping in unlocked cars with nothing but a medium-thick jacket as a blanket. I hate the cold, ever since I was born a blue-lipped shivering baby, just a bit more than four pounds. Fuck this shit. Time to head south where it's warmer. LA? San Diego? Join the rebels in Chiapas? These are the things that occupy my mind as I delinquently forage for coffee to wake and warm my dirty ass up with.

I see a rocker downtown that I know, and he tells me a terrible thing has happened. Lynn Strait was killed yesterday with his dog after being t-boned by a truck down by Rincon. There's a weird janky spot where you expose yourself to the traffic, and the sun gets in your eyes as you're making the turn across lanes. *Bam!* Gone in an instant.

All that talent that was just starting to get recognized. Lynn was the singer for Snot with Mikey from Kronyx playing guitar, and they were killing it, getting on the Geffen label as the freshest faces of *nu-core* metal. Think Korn or Deftones but with a melodic nitrousy twang. Or maybe a Sublime meets Rage Against the Machine? Lynn was a natural frontman, jumping around and stomping like a mad man, screaming into the microphone until foam flew out his mouth onto the unruly crowd. He had paid his dues playing bass guitar for Lethal Dose, and now was his time to spread his peacock feathers.

I had only gotten a chance to see them a few times as they had already outgrown our small hamlet that seems to produce so much talent at everything that is cool. They are off in LA all the time now, even Ozzfest recently. It looked like things were going to be smooth sailing to the rest of us. We were proud.

Lynn was a real junkyard dog looking motherfucker when you saw him strut towards you from across the pit floor in his wife-beater with his *fuck it all* slouch, piercings as thick as your pinky wagging in his ears. When he got close, you saw that he was actually handsome. There are two things kids that grew up in Santa Barbara aren't ever short on, tragedy... and looks.

He had a wide boxer's jaw and chin. You can see a bit of poetic melancholy in his slightly droopy eyes. On top of the eyes sat the furrowed and pronounced brow of a battle-ready Viking. Under it all was a big beautiful smile that showed off the robust lips of a lover boy. The eclectic juxtaposition of all these features and accessories is a good example of his internal double blade: the lovable criminal, the sweet and the savage. To go with that boxer's face was his boxer dog, Dobbs. That dog is on the cover of *Get Some*, what would be the only album Lynn would make with Snot. Rest in peace to you too, Dobbs. I'm glad it was quick. December 11th, 1998. Shitty day. The worst. I'm devastated.

I sit on a bench on State Street, even abandoning my coffee mission. I think of the time Lynn protected me from a bully about 10 years ago. I was in a conversation circle of people at a keg party in Isla Vista, and I see someone that owes me $20. I know they have it because they are intentionally dressed like a peasant. That's how you know a guy has at least a quarter ounce of green bud on him. Shabby clothes, even though he usually wears the newest Quicksilver. That *Oliver Twist* look on his face. Jackpot!

I call it "Monk Robe Strategy." The more you actually have, the less you need to appear that you have; otherwise, these vultures will tear you apart. Ha, I invented "Monk Robe," you *hoser-ass-Billy*. I make a beeline towards him. He's wearing a hooded sweatshirt with the sleeves cut off and some old board shorts with guacamole stains. *Oh yeah, he's high rolling.* I notice a bulge in his cargo pocket area. Got you, fuck face. I approach from just out of his periphery so I can roll up and snake the sack.

Just before I get there, *wham!*—not the band, it's a blow to my nuts. It's Brad, and he's just kicked my balls up into my throat. For what, I don't know. I drop to my knees, and a few people groan in sympathy. Brad laughs and disappears into the crowd. Lynn comes up and yells after Brad, "Don't be an asshole!" Mikey from Kronyx is still partially doubled over in an empathetic co-feel. Lynn asks if I am ok, and lifts me back to my feet.

"I'm good," I wheeze, pretending it's nothing.

"Don't let him get away with that. You have to try to fuck him up, even if you lose."

"Well, I'm trying to pick up the pieces of my nuts at the moment," I say through shallow, desperately slurped breaths.

"I would have helped you, but I'm holding a beer, bro. That's sucks," goes Mikey.

"All right. That guy's a little bitch. You could probably kick his ass," says Lynn, with an encouraging shoulder shake and a look of genuine concern.

"Ok, Lynn. I will," I lie.

There are always guys like Brad you have to watch out for. They are too ugly, stupid, and mean for any girls to make out with them. He's surrounded by all this miraculous early womanhood. They're just waiting for you to be the least bit tolerable, and he can't even pull it off. I imagine that is about the most frustrating thing that can happen to a guy. Everyone around you is fucking, and all you have is your sad, tired ass hand. Mostly these negative game having guys just bottle it up and sit miserably at the edge of the party, drinking themselves into oblivion, so they don't have to think about what's wrong with them. Their obsession with that question only makes the problem worse. A pussyless spiral into hell, their cocks slowly twisting into potentially hateful rape clubs.

Brad, the pussyless bully, hates me just for being handsome, which I am, in a kind of a James Franco/Paul Newman type of way with .04% body fat. He sees that I'm ok with the ladies, making them laugh all the time. It angers him. He is older and bigger and thumps me because he can.

Lynn at least gave a shit. That helps. It might not seem like much to you, but in the jungle, that's as close as you get to unadulterated affection and empathy. I guess when you look like a pierced, tattooed junkyard dog, you can show a little heart without being called a pussy. It meant a lot to me when I was 16. I never forgot it, and it made me feel stronger. I would be an ass-kicker soon enough. I guess I always was a bit sensitive in the beginning until the world made me see the flaw in that. Until it *Kevlared* my heart. And now Lynn is dead. Fuck. There's clearly still some heart in there because it hurts right now.

I remember another, far more recent story about him when Snot performed at Ozzfest:

Limp Bizkit is on stage, and they have a 12-foot toilet up there as a prop. Snot has already played, and Lynn pops out of the toilet naked, and a chick runs up and starts lapping at Lynn's balls and dick in front of 10,000 people. On top of a giant toilet! She's a real specialist, and it appears Lynn is game to let her finish the job. Limp Bizkit plays on for the delight of Lynn's biscuit, which is becoming very unlimp.

Unfortunately, security has other ideas. No one wants to tackle the naked guy first, though, and Lynn is able to scramble into Ozzy's dressing room, where Ozzy's wife Sharon is. He's all, "Sharon! You haven't met me yet, but the cops are coming. Hide me!"

I assume even music industry wizened Sharon Osbourne's head exploded at that point. She promised she would help him, but Lynn ended up in jail anyway, booked in under the fake name of Dave Mustaine—singer of Megadeath.

Why'd you rat him out, Sharon? Not very metal! Not very metal at all. Another classic Santa Barbara boy gone too soon. Rest in peace, you fucking savage.

Ouch!

At this point, I only come out at night, and I am starting to look like a vampire. I finally say, *fuck the money*. I am becoming a different person than who I used to be. I used to be good. Reckless, but good. Like a poetic public pranker whose message is an inspirational riddle. I've been lucky enough to get away with this for a while now. I still have a year on my felony probation, and I'm going to go legit. Or maybe I'll just go to a country where my record is cleaner. Let's be realistic. But first, I want to flee town with some irresponsible flamboyance.

I've gotten in pretty deep at this point, so it promises to be a beautiful bus crash. So, I'm trying to score some crack with Alex, right?—'wait, what?' you ask?– Yeah, Alex, while seeming to be a big-time nerd, will do any drug at any time. **Except** for hallucinogens, which always send him on a bad trip because his complicated brain is a horror show. He really likes to take stimulants, sit silently in a corner at the house party, smiling, and rocking his head back and forth. He's only smiling at one of two possible things, that Rita will atone for her sexual missteps and become a *born-again virgin*, or the infinite beauty and predictability of math.

Someone got this motherfucker some crack recently, and the last few Saturdays he's been dangling multiple $20 bills at me after the bars close. Our recent running agreement is that I go score it, and he gives up the cash. Sweet deal for me, right? Yeah, until I get rolled and smacked in the lip with the butt of a gun. Not hard enough to break a tooth, but hard enough to make it clear that I should *fuck off*. So, I go back to where Alex is waiting in safety, and he sees my lip gushing blood, and out of great concern says, "Oh my God, J.C.?! You didn't get the shit!?"

As if that isn't bad enough, we go call this 300-pound heroin dealer and have her bring over some heroin and cocaine. So, there I am, looking over my huge bloody lip, at a 300-pound heroin dealer, shooting me up with a speedball! The revolting picture starts to nauseate me, but then the coke hits me…then the heroin. Then I remember suddenly thinking the heroin dealer is *beautiful in her own way*. She smiles at me, and I give her a gob of Alex's money and forget to get the change.

The next morning all I can think about is the horrible picture of the bloody lip and the fat woman slamming my vein with a speedball. I look shamefully at the needle mark in my arm and wonder how much of a herpes sore my smashed open lip is looking like. For the first time, I feel like maybe life isn't going to work out after all.

All my anger from the boxing match is gone. Now I just feel self-pity and contempt for people who have it so easy. Maybe I am just low-class debris like so many say. Then I do get mad, but not at my perceived enemies. I get mad at myself for a change. I think it's my 16yo self that is yelling, actually. He had never lost faith in himself through the group home. Or through the degradation of watching his mother get treated without regard or respect as she struggles to feed her three children. She raised them in a teepee, while he, the 14yo man of the family, had to watch almost helplessly.

He had always believed in himself. All the way from when he left the teepee to go out in the world. When he'd hoped to make a fortune and vindicate his family. To provide them safety. And now, ten years later, no fortune, no vindication, not even any self-respect. My 16yo self isn't going to let his memory get besmirched by this fool! He starts yelling, "Oh, look at the poor little pussy shot up a speedball, and now he wants to go jump in the river! You're pathetic! Do you know that? To think that I became you! Fuckin' get out of town! That's all you need is a vacation. A permanent vacation from this piece of shit town. Fuckin' go! What are you waiting for? Go!"

So, I did. I crammed some clothes in a duffel bag and threw pretty much everything else I owned next to a trashcan so a bum could get it. And that was it, man. I was out.

Hey, Yo...Mexico

After a quick visit to San Diego with my perpetual savior Laduska, I ask her and her boyfriend Mixt to drop me off on the Tijuana border. She is wary of dropping me off there with little money and even less of a plan. She says, "Why don't you play bass in our band? We're going on tour. We'll give you a crash-course lesson wise. "

"We do need a bass player. It's easy." Says Mixt, "You just twang it with the music. *Twang!*" He'll be playing guitar, and singing along with Laduska.

Three people in a van going cross country, playing music? It could be fun. But no, I'm being called south. Shit. I wait years for an excuse to get out of Santa Barbara, and now there are two at once? Yay/boo?

Laduska is a pretty blonde girl that is just the portrait of kindness. Her morals are higher than her cheekbones. Piercing blues and an easy laugh that you'd know a block away. What she's doing looking after scallywags like me, I'll never know. Her smile can cure depression guaranteed for 6-8 weeks. I'd a tried to marry her years ago, but she's just too pure.

I wouldn't want her to have to try and explain me to the other angels. She has a slight rasp in her voice from riding her bike into a clothesline with her neck at 9yo.

She rolls to the party, looking to have fun in an aggressive fashion. She's on the team. I love this girl, and if Laduska ever told me she had a problem with someone, I wouldn't even ask what it was about. I'd already know *they* were wrong. I'd just need to know what she thought the punishment should be, then I'd secretly double it because she's a softy.

She's finally putting her band together. She's going to be drumming and co-singing. I remember she'd just bang on shit at people's house parties with these drum sticks. She'd be playing AC/DC on some motorcycle helmets, fireplace mantles, or maybe an urn with some ashes in it. *Bang! Bodda!Boot!Boot!Dingily!Ding!Ding!Doot!*

They're calling the band Flooded. I'm honored to be asked, but I gotta be honest, I've never played an instrument. That's not exactly true, I have tried. It's like the thing shriveled and twisted to get away from me, going, *"This is NOT for you!"* Weird behavior for a harmonica.

So, I try to turn down the exciting offer with some grace. "I don't think Boise deserves that, guys. I love music. You know I do. But my fingers are allergic to instruments. I suck. Thanks for the ride, though, you guys. Don't worry, I'll be in Puerto Vallarta after a few naps on a bus. I'll see you in a few months. You guys will find a bass player."—they do too. A little leprechaun named Garvey. They had to pick someone small so they could all three sleep on the floor of the tour van once they hit the road.

I hop out before anyone gets misty-eyed, and I walk across the border, get to the station, and get a ticket for Puerto Vallarta. I can only afford the third-class ticket. How bad could it be, right? I've been to the skid row Greyhound station in LA. I doubt it can be worse than that.

I decide I'm going to write a screenplay while I'm down here. This will be my purpose in life, to tell stories *and* make a million bucks while I do it. That's where I get my first inspiration to write stories down, instead of just telling them to drunk people who only pay in beer and forget two minutes later. Right here in the Tijuana bus station, I decide to be a serious writer for the first time.

There has been drunk talk about writing scripts and making movies, sure. But drunk talk is worse than doing nothing at all. It admits there's a desire that something should be done, and it pretends that if enough bullshit gets spewed all over the ground tonight, maybe it'll act as fertilizer for the seeds of our dreams.

The ride lasts three days and two nights. No air conditioning. By the second day, it starts smelling more like a Greyhound in here, stopping at every little town in the Sonoran goddamn Desert. I'm ready to buy a first-class ticket. "Are we ahead of the first-class bus? Could I wait here for it? How do you say that in Spanish?"

I decide I better not be a nuisance, or the driver will be like, "Oh, yes, *Amigo. Uno momento.* Eeet's right behind us. You wait here." I'm not falling for *that* trick.

At three in the morning on the second night, the bus gets boarded by soldiers saying we have to get off the bus. What the hell are they talking about? I'm the only white boy on the bus. This should be *not awesome.* I grab my duffel bag as directed and stumble out to the bright florescent lights of the desert military checkpoint. Then, a whiff of hot desert air that doesn't seem to give you enough oxygen comes crinkling into my sinuses, which are still chalked and chafed from a year—or two?—of regular cocaine use.

This is probably the first weekend I won't be doing coke in a while, and I'm sure I don't have a look of eager anticipation on my face, especially with the lights and the soldiers making me paranoid. What if they shine a flashlight up my nose? We file up in a line, and I seem like I'm the only one that isn't prepared for this. The person at the front of the line presses a button, and it's just like a crosswalk. If you get the green light, you go back on the bus. If you get red, like I do, you go to the other line, where you get to empty out your bag.

Oh man, I tied the green military duffel bag off in a knot at the top, and the shit got tight, and I've been sleeping with my arms all folded up underneath me twisted up in a flannel under my neck. As a result, my hands have fallen asleep. Now I'm having trouble getting the knot open. So, this soldier pulls out this hedge-clipper type thing and clips the non-government issue rope that was replaced sometime after WWII and will now have to be replaced again.

All I have in this bag are some books and clothes, most of which are dirty. Very dirty. I start slowing down so as to not have to pull out the dirty socks, and the Mexican Army man gives me a wave to get back on the bus after he gets a preview whiff. I walk away, clasping the top of the bag with my sleepy hands. I wonder how many white boys they catch smuggling drugs *down* the continent—yeah, them farmers down in Chiapas will pay $75 an eighth—I think the soldiers saw my duffel bag and thought I was an American soldier. They wanted to kind of say, "America-shmerica. You ain't got no B-1 bomber down here. You're in The Sonora now, boy!"

Beachside Jalisco

After a long grueling ride through the Sonoran Desert and Sinaloa, my memory of Greyhound grows a bit fonder. We finally arrive in Puerto Vallarta. *Oh, what a difference a desert makes.* I stretch out my achy muscles on the coarsely sanded beach and dive into the epic blue water to wash the 3-day grime of the bus off me. It is quite renewing. The energy of both myself and Puerto Vallarta is upbeat and optimistic. Liz Taylor had a big house built here in the 60s when it was just a little fishing village. Now they have a Hooters.

A kid with a straw-hat wanders by with two huge gourds full of icy *tamarindo agua fresca*. The gourds hang down either side of him from a stick that runs across his shoulders. I buy a cold glass to drink. It's dust in a half-second, and the boy is there with several more. At 50-cents a pop, just leave me one of the gourds and come back later when it's empty.

This place looks like the opposite of the open-air vice market that is Tijuana, which, like many Californians, is the only place in Mexico I had ever been to before. The real truth is that the Tijuana border is the sphincter that Mexico rams its giant narcotic dick into America with.

And America loves it. It begs for it. But since the ramming never stops, the outside of America's butthole, Tijuana, is very untidy. The idea that a vast country such as Mexico may offer a bit of diversity has so far been lost on my pompous and presumptuous American mind. Note taken. It's like a tropical paradise down here. Green hills, with enough flat area for a town, up against a nice long beach that edges a deep blue sea.

I sit in the sand and try to figure out what I should do next with my minimal pesos. My brother, mom, and sister are already down here. I'm supposed to meet them tomorrow at a predetermined landmark. It should be easy to find because I've seen it before, yet I have never been there. Puerto Vallarta is the sister city to Santa Barbara, and they have an identical famous dolphin fountain to ours. Right down by the beach. We're to meet there at noon. Easy-peasy

I get the cheapest hotel possible for the night, and at $5, you can bet that it is quite shabby. I get a small electric shock turning on the light, and there is water dripping from the ceiling in the corner of the room. At least it's not over the bed. Down with the drips come little snowflakes spiraling slowly and diagonally down. I assume these are made of asbestos. It's definitely not paint. There are long black hairs on the pillowcase of the paper-thin pillow they have offered me on the lumpy, ancient twin bed that when you lie on it, you can count the mattress springs corkscrewing their way into your back. The wool blanket feels like a scouring pad and smells like maybe a few people have died on it. Despite all this, I fall into the bed as if I'm floating in a sensory deprivation tank on Quaaludes.

My last conscious thought is to the last time I had almost been asleep on the bus. A chicken jumped on top of my head, cranium hopscotching towards the front door. Ever since they named him 'Taco,' he knew what their plans were, and now was his chance to make a break for it. His plan to live worked about as good as mine to sleep.

And now, here is an actual bed, terrible as it may be. For 12 hours, I dream dreams of happiness and celebration. Surfing, dancing, I think, even a flying dream. I am away from Santa Barbara, the beautiful temptress who was destroying me. Now I'm in an exotic land, here to make a new start!

I have a mission to write a screenplay about a musician who fakes his death to escape the inevitable lameness of fame. Perhaps a possible alternative ending to Kurt Cobain's tragic life? The David Geffen provided safehouse/resort has all the amenities. *But wait, there's an evil professor!* The screenplay will be called Giancarlo's Dead, after our friend, the legendary bearded and dreadlocked, gravelly throated guitar player, and singer of the band, Creature Feature.

When I go to meet Auggie, Mom, and Hannah, I realize I'm a day early. I'm sitting here at this dolphin fountain for two hours before I realize that it's Saturday and not Sunday. The endless bus trip made me lose track. Shit. I just spent the last of my money on luxurious fresh-squeezed orange juice, coffee, eggs, refried beans, and tortillas.

I head up the river Quale away from where it empties into the ocean, towards the neighborhoods where the locals who wait on the beach tourists live. Up near a bridge that connects the two sides of town that the river dissects is an open-air swap meet where I feel like I could hustle up enough money to survive the next 24 hours. I know Auggie will have some sort of business running that I can jump on to get me started. He's been a business genius since he was five. I'm not too worried about things beyond the here and now. Just gotta get a couple of hundred pesos going somehow.

What do I have to sell? Japanese electronics are more valuable in Mexico, so I guess it's going to be my Walkman and all the cassette tapes. They were critical in getting through that three-day bus ride, but that's all in the past. Time to save my ass twice, cassette player. Let's see, I've got Soundgarden, Sabbath, Public Enemy, Suicidal Tendencies, Mother Love Bone, Cat Stevens, The Police, U2, and Blondie. A pretty good collection, really. It shows a bit of a lack in my taste development since this is mostly stuff I've been listening to since I was a teen. Good shit is good shit though, am I right?

The batteries just went through a giant desert and are probably about as worn out as me, but for now, they work. I'm going to pretend they are new for a bit of leverage since this kid is going to weasel me down on account of we are in his territory. Also, I wouldn't be trying to sell this at a swap meet if I didn't *really* need the money. He tests it out. He hears the grinding guitar and howling voice go from werewolf growl to prison yard siren, and he smiles. *"Cuanto?"* he says.

"Veinte Americano," ($20 US) I respond, surprised he allows me the open. What kind of swap meet rat are you, kid? I had worked the swap meets of the Inland Empire with my dad during the summers of Reagan. He would have slapped me in the back of the head for not instantly low-balling.

The kid looks at his dad, who is looking around the street to see if there are any serious buyers of t-shirts, Guatemalan bracelets, or flip flops left out there. It's what, as a future film director, I would call *the magic hour.* Suitable for film making. Swap meets? Not so much. Time to start thinking about wrapping it up. Papa asks how much, now drawn in from the side. "Cuanto?"

"Veinte. Mucho cassettas! Por favor, Papa," he begs.

"No," says dad.

"The batteries work good." I offer. "Energ-i-zer."

"*PAPA!*" the kid starts squealing.

Amazing, I think. These guys have the fanciest trinket stand in the row, and now it's clear the kid is a spoiled little chubby fucker. I should have started at $30. Now, dad is trying to come in as the *bad cop*, which is smart, but I know that he knows his life will be ruined for the rest of the day if I walk away with this Walkman. The kid has been poorly trained for the swap meet hustle. I feel bad for the transaction burden he must be to his father on Saturdays and Sundays. Maybe Mom is sick or something, Dad had to drag him along. I should have started at $30. Idiot!

"*Diez,*" says father, having now walked over and is inspecting the goods with an uninvested loose wrist as if he's just going through the motions to say "No" again.

"Ten?" I laugh at this. "*Veinte.* I paid that much just for the tapes. Look. Ozzy Osbourne. *Mira. Bueno Calidad.*" I only know restaurant and cocaine dealing Spanish because I'm a typical Cali-beach town-dive bar rat. This seems to be enough to get my point across, however, along with English words such as Ozzy Osbourne, which most Mexicans understand. I've got this.

"*PAPA!!* Asi Osbourne!" the kid starts having a meltdown.

"*Carajo!*" Dad submits. He pulls out his giant chained leather wallet and counts out the pesos to almost the proportionate amount. Fucker is loaded, I blew it.

I immediately buy a pint of Cazadores Tequila and go to the restaurant and order half a roasted chicken with two Negro Modelos and all the accouterments. Ah, look at that, freshly pressed corn tortillas, cilantro, onion, hot sauce, *pico de gallo*, that crumbly white farm cheese, beans. All served on big, hand-painted, red, clay plates. After that, I have enough left for another night in the hotel and a few beers at a bar. I hustle some Canadian tourists at pool, and I'm able to wake up with a decent hangover and enough money for terrible coffee and a single, orange-yolked fried egg on top of some *chilaquiles*. God, can someone please get Mexico some decent coffee? How the fuck are they so productive drinking this shit?

It's finally time to meet the family at the fountain, and everyone looks fairly happy and vibrant. I think Santa Barbara had been wearing on all of them as well. A new adventure is just the ticket! We have lunch and all take a bus back to the village they are living in, Nagolito.

We have a house, but there's a catch. They're still building it. The concrete and brick exteriors are finished, and now the workers are just focused on the interior. Mom has decided that there is no reason we shouldn't just live outside, up on the flat, concrete roof. She is planning on living up there anyway, so really, it's just us kids that are waiting for a toilet, shower, and kitchen. The weather is nice enough to sleep outside—*I thought my hole shitting days were over, Mom!*—she loves getting you way out in nature and making you use a leaf for toilet paper. I can almost hear her laughing two bushes over—*fuck this shit, Mom! I'm a **fancy** wandering slut now.*

The workers show up and shake their heads at the crazy Americans up on the roof before they go into the interior to finalize some details. Even the Australians across the street think we're hardcore, and that is saying something. Not city types either, they are from Darwin, and I end up over at their campfire some evenings. They think I'm quite a character and pass me drinks of cheap tequila to keep me talking past midnight.

The village seems like a bit of an afterthought, with all manners of housing structures built here and there. There's an electric plant humming loudly in the distance. Everyone from direct Mayan descendants to Australian backpackers, hardy German tourists, ex-pat Americans trying to stretch their shitty Social Security checks, mangy dogs. We're all hanging around wondering where the closest place to have fun outside of this dust bowl is. The rent is cheap, but this shit is bullshit. The stream that runs through this place has rainbow-colored films globbing up on its edges that seem like they're composed of a more nefarious material than soap. There's a small store made of plywood that is open when it feels like it. The sun blazes down, and the dust rises up whenever a car drives by.

We are towards the front of the village near the main road, so cars do drive by quite often. Even a mule-drawn cart can implant a decent-sized mud-booger up your nostril. They all try to go slow and keep the dust down but inevitably fail. It might be they are just trying to get a look at the crazy Americans living on the roof of a half-built house.

The Chicken Story

I ride the bus into Puerto Vallarta on most days. The driver drives like he's on peyote down the twisty road, death on one side of us, unpredictable oncoming traffic on the other. It's only 12 pesos, so I'm not complaining. Once I get off the bus, I realize I'm too big for the narrow sidewalks. The traffic is just blazing by, daring me to try to step around a group of ladies with bundles tied to their heads.

Right there in downtown, there are Indians with bundles tied around their heads, protruding a foot to either side, bumping me aside. Cars zipping by with stuff tied to the top of them, hanging my direction too, threatening to take me out even as I walk on the sidewalk. I realize that I'm going to either have to crouch down to *sub-bundle level* or start hop-scotching Indians to make any progress. Luckily, it's just the morning rush, and things suddenly calm down a little bit before I'm decapitated by a bed frame rail.

As I drink my coffee, I watch as a guy's red chicken gets away from him and runs into traffic. A big truck comes rolling up and *pop!* I think that's a weird sound for a chicken's last sound to be, but that's what it was. The guy just looks at his chicken and slumps his shoulders from the edge of the curb. I remember wishing he'd turn a little more my way so I could get more of a side profile view of his face. I think it would have probably made a great painting, *He wasn't dinner, he was my Brother.*

The guy just walks away after a second, leaving the chicken laying there. Another guy with a cowboy hat picks up the chicken and goes after him, holding it up to show him it's ok; its heart has just popped out the chest. His assertion meets only the other man's back as it walks away from him.

He shrugs his shoulders, and he walks away with the upside-down chicken in his hand, determined it not die in vain. Its wings spread in the Jesus Christ pose, tips gently bobbing as if floating on a bubbly current up to chicken heaven. The scene is over, leaving nothing but a little spot of red where the tires are passing over. The tailpipes gush black smoke into the blood. Welcome to Mexico, *gringo.*

Prabhu Prakash

I finish my chicory and coffee blend and go meet Auggie, Mom, and Hannah. After a nice walk around the touristy part of town, we go to this temple, where Auggie is tending vegetables out of a strip of dirt they're lending him for a percentage of the harvest.

When we get there, I'm amazed at this place. There's a big iron gate, a winding cobblestone path up a big hill through mango and apple trees. At the top is a great adobe and red tile mansion with incense and rock and roll music coming out of it. I look at my brother and say, "Is that Nina Hagen?"

"Yeah, probably. These guys are awesome. They welcome non-traditional influences," says Auggie.

I'm amazed and also not that he's already nestled up into the most beautiful mansion in town. A religious one, but still. Nina Hagen? Maybe there *is* hope for some religious people. Let's see.

The first person I meet is Prabhu Prakash, the spiritual head honcho.

He's got these enormous eyes. Real bright, big, friendly, and hypnotizing. He is an old skinny Mexican guy wearing a robe and carrying a plain walking stick. He hasn't got much hair except for his salt 'n' pepper beard. He's working on the midday meal all by himself. I go in and help him while Auggie is checking out the garden.

I am sitting there watching, and everyone else is busy doing other chores, so I'm like, *"Necesito ayuda?"* The words that I'm pretty sure mean, "You need some help, bro?"

"Si," he says, and then he grabs my forearm gently, and he leads me to a cutting board where he gets me chopping.

After that, I return every day for months as Prabhu's assistant cook at the Krishna temple, eventually living there at the temple along with Auggie, Mom, and Hannah. Prabhu is almost blind from being diabetic and not believing in insulin. This makes him bone-thin too. He's unsteady as he walks with his stick, but once Prabhu plants himself in front of you, it gives you the impression that he's as firmly planted as a little manzanita bush, out of which two focused eyes pierce the fuzz you are to them.

Fuzz is just chakra levels to Prabhu. He says mine are ok but need some work time in the kitchen. At least I think that's what he said. He doesn't speak much English. I think he speaks 40 words to my 60 of Spanish. You would be surprised how much two guys can communicate with 100 words, hand motions, and eye gestures.

Prabhu puts simple stories into it like there's a way to cut the tomato that would explain to it that we are sorry to cause it any discomfort, but we are going to send it to the next level of reincarnation now. Then Prabhu picks up the onion and says, *"Ceboyya, Whoosteeen."*

So, I take this to mean that I am supposed to tell the tomato, "The next level for <u>tomato</u> is onion, see?" Then I show the onion to the tomato so the tomato can see what he is going to *become* and to show the onion what he had *been*. But there is a level between your next life, Mr. Onion, and Mr. Tomato. It's called SALSA!!" *Chop! Choppity-chop-chop-chop!*

Prabhu looks over and sees me talking to the vegetables and says, "Si, Whooooosteen. Buenas verduras! Buenas verduras!"

Each vegetable had its own way to be sent into its next self. The purple onions were to be chopped in half down the equator and held back together like a big purple airplane wheel. Then, the razor-sharp knife goes in under the thumb webbing, and two half-inch rings are cut, plucked out quickly, repeat. In the end, you can't leave much of a butt on the onion for waste considerations. It affects your next life if your demise is wasted on *nothing* in any way. You also need 6-8 equally thick slices of onion by the time you're done slicing.

That's just the first stage, each recipe requires different sizes, shapes, and cuts. It's very complicated. I think Prabhu is going to be a chemist in his next life. Of course, what is cooking but practical chemistry mixed with an equal amount of spontaneous instinct, right?

One day Prabhu looks over and says, *"Gracias, Whhooosteeen. Prabhu's Ojos, es no Bueno."*

And I think, *Wait, I know how to answer this in Spanish. He said his eyes don't work too good.* So, I say, *"Es no problema, Prabhu. Ojos de la Corazon es mas importante,"* which almost means, "It's not a problem Prabhu because the eyes of the heart are more important."

He looks at me and smiles. He has such a great smile and a little, *"Tee-hee-hee,"* giggle. *"Tee-hee-hee, si Whosteeeen."* He loves me, and I love him. They've never pressured me to be a Krishna or anything, and I've never expressed any desire to be one, outside of doing the Hari Rama chants with them sometimes to show that I have no distaste for Krishna. Which I don't necessarily. It's the Catholics I'm mostly after.

Now, as I said before, these people have a lot of different influences going on. They have rock and roll on the radio, pictures of the Virgin Mary on the walls, six-armed elephant statuettes on the ground, Nag Champa incense in the air, and weed in their brains. That's right, weed. They have it, they love it. The Mayberry pole all these peace ribbons are tied to is Krishna. Some churches are based on goodwill. I guess it depends on the management. Fraudsters love religion because it's based on blind trust. That's why it's especially important to be careful who you pick as a preacher. My recommendation is to be your own preacher if you **really** feel you need one. It's all bullshit anyway, but whatever relaxes you. Don't tell Prabhu I said that. If I had to pick a preacher, it'd be him. Tell him that as a consolation if he presses you.

Here's something crazy you might have forgotten. I passed over it before. Prabhu is dying from a lack of insulin. I try to talk sense into him. "Ride both lanes, Prabhu. Don't let Krishna turn off all the other burners on the stove. I mean, if you've modified the religion to accept the music of Nina Hagen, is a syringe full of insulin that much different? I mean, Nina Hagen? Syringe? Come on, Prabhu."

Prabhu just looks at me, confused and annoyed, pretending not to understand at all, then, like he suddenly has something to do in the kitchen. He dramatically stamps out the half roasted joint in the ashtray, signaling the end of break time and *loss of further joint privileges* until after dinner.

I give up because it seems like people have tried to tell him this stuff before.

I can't help think and hope that he picks me up on the ESP level. I project and focus my brain like a laser to needle the shit into his brain >>Bullshit, Prabhu. You're sentencing yourself to death, and I can see people around here love you. For a religion? You seem smarter than that Prabhu. Your boy, Gandhi? When his wife got pneumonia? He'd only let her have water from the polluted Ganges River. Yuk. That was his big cure—on the basis of his r-e-l-i-g-i-o-n... He wouldn't let her take western medicine, and she died. Then, when **he** got malaria? He went running for that shit. That's right, Prabhu. Your boy Gandhi was all, "Down the hatch! Thanks, white doctor!" Wake up, dude!<<

Of course, I can't say this part out loud, or I would probably get kicked out of the temple. Prabhu knows, though. I put that shit **right** in. his. brain.

This guy is so skinny I can see his heart beating through his linen robe. His fuckin' eyes are sunken into the sockets, and his temples are bony too. The eyes, though, the eyes are the healthiest things I have ever seen. So, what do I know? Maybe he's onto something. I don't push it too much, he forgets about it, and life goes on at the temple.

Each story I hear Prabhu Prakash tell strangers is peppered with kind words I know like, *"Amor,"* *"Tranquilo,"* and especially, *"Krishna."* I like to just watch him talk to people. He's authoritative, yet gentle. He would give CPR to a rabid Komodo dragon if he could. He stops who he's talking to and looks over at me occasionally and says, *"Si, Whhooosteeen?"* to keep me involved. He calls me, *"Whhooosteeen,"* all slow and drawn out. It's fucking adorable, and I say, *"Si, Prakash,"* like I know what the hell he's talking about.

Off to the side of the conversation, I keep dumping a plastic bucket of water over the temple's "guard dog," Corneto. It's time for his monthly shower. Corneto is a lazy Doberman Pincher with uncut ears that likes to nestle up next to Prabhu when it's joint smoking time. This old dog likes to get that *Scooby-Doo contact high.* As far as Mexican dogs go, he doesn't look too shitty besides being pretty joint stiff, dingy, and old.

Angel loves that dog, and I'm glad I won't be here to see the tears in that little long-haired Mayan's face when old Corneto kicks the bucket. They will give him a hero's burial when he does. As a guard dog, Corneto wouldn't bark at an intruder if they kicked him in the ribs. I imagine they'll plant some bushes over his carcass so he can come back as flowers. I wouldn't mind that myself. Put me belly-down in that hole in a *flying dream* pose so I can look down and smile at the river. Get some roses growin' outta my b-hole. That'd be funny.

Few English-speaking people visit the temple. This gives me plenty of free time to cruise around, write my screenplay out on the kitchen porch, and gaze down at the river *Cuale'.* The little river wraps around the base of the hill the temple is perched atop just outside Puerto Vallarta, in a little town called Romantica.

Little girls wash their clothes down there where the good drying rocks are. In the same crook of the river, their *abuelas* used to wash *their* socks.

Angel lives in the room with Prabhu. He's a young Indian who came from the lower part of the country where the people are shorter, and the food is better. He goes to school in the day and is in charge of bringing home weed, which Prabhu loves. It helps kill the pain from dying of untreated diabetes. Now, I am baffled why he won't shoot up insulin, but he will smoke weed. "Could we grind it up in his food or something?"

I don't think I've impressed enough before that this man is wasting away, and I hear he was the size of a normal man just a few years ago. "Is it because of money, Angel?"

"No, temple has money," Angel, the student from the countryside, says solemnly.

"Well, it's his choice. Sad," I resignedly declare. Angel sighs, in joined sadness. He thinks Prabhu is being stubborn too.

Prabhu now has a colossal joint in his mouth and is rocking his head up and down on his foam rubber mattress to a heavy metal Krishna band. The angst-filled guitar riffs bounce high up amongst the spider webs in the high adobe interior and back down again. I watch these people dust and sweep the temple around spider webs so as not to disturb their brothers. One day when they ask me to sweep, I take it as a great honor.

Prabhu smokes a lot of weed in the evenings, I think that's when the pain comes. Prabhu sends me to the store to get the stuff we need for dinner, and I hit the street in my new purple and brown sheet fabric peasant clothes. Mom made them for the whole family. Different colors for each person. Pretty dope.

Ma's Doin' OK

It's nice to see Mom thriving down here in Mexico. The vertical stress creases on her face have softened up a bit, and she even smiles sometimes, staying active with some projects of her own around town. My entire goal in life is to get enough money to buy her a piece of property somewhere so she can plant her gardens, cook pies, and tend the animals without worrying if the cops will come bust up the camp.

The world has shown my poor mother about as much sympathy as any other mom who didn't have the experience to test a man well enough before making the big decision. The decision to have a kid with him, only to be left alone in the end, thinking, *Well, I'll work hard while the kids are at school, and the oldest one can watch the youngest one while I moonlight at the 24-hour diner. Under the table, of course, so as not to jeopardize the meager $700 welfare check. I guess that will allow the manager to try and get creepy on me since he is keeping secrets for me. Oh well, I'll fend him off for the kids. Gotta put up with a little shit sometimes for the kids.*

My mom did all of this while going to college to get us out of the welfare hole. But that's not the incredible part, the astonishing part is, as every welfare mother knows, how the world will just dump piles of crap onto you as you so valiantly attempt this.

By age seven, I had watched a dozen black-hearted government bureaucrats talk to my heroic mother like she was a borderline criminal. Tossing out a beyond condescending, "And the food stamps I've given you? Have they been going to feed the children?" As if he's pulling the food stamps out of his own savings account. *Fuck you, Larry, the law school dropout turned social worker.* Ma lets them have it too. "No! I have to turn everything over to my pimp! Of course, they feed the children!"

By 12, I had watched tons of predatorial men try to pick up my mother under the guise of, "Let's get your kids some deep-fried shrimp at Long John Silver's." After a while, she figured it out, and we just didn't end up at Long John Silver's anymore.

By the time I was 16, I was mad at the world and punching people out all the time. By the time I got tossed in the group home, she had been through too many years of shit, and one day she just nonchalantly announced, "Pack your stuff, we're moving outside." And that's what my mom, brother, and sister did. They watched our mother build with eucalyptus bark, branches, and twine, a teepee. And we *lived* in that motherfucker.

Right at the point where I was thinking about making out with girls, my mom was like, "Yeah, about that?"

My mom proceeded to buy my sister all kinds of farm animals because she was still young enough to create an illusory fantasy world for. "It's not bein' homeless, it's a permanent unicorn slumber party!"

So, as you can see, we are an eccentric bunch. Some people don't like our style; but the ones that do, really do. It's nice to see Mom not trying to challenge the local attitudes and politics for once. "People aren't trying to play mental manipulation chess games on you all the time down here," declares mom, not realizing they're probably still gossiping about her, she just can't understand it.

"Yeah, Mom. It is a simpler life. Everyone's too busy with day to day survival to sit and talk about the neighbors too much."

The fresh start down here has done us all good. Sometimes you just need a new town, man. People in America are too scared to take the big risk and move to a new city once they're in their 30s. That's how long being alive usually seems to take to crush a guy's imagination and wonder. Until about your 30s. Not us, though. We bounced out of judgment town. We're squeaky clean and listenin' to Ween!

Jalisco Dogs

On the way to get Jalisco's equivalent to mozzarella cheese and tomato sauce for Hari Krishna pizza, I see something extraordinary outside the store. A dog has its penis stuck in another dog and is panicking, trying to get it out. I mean, this guy looks nervous, and then I realize why. A group of kids gathers up instantly, and they're now taunting the botched pair of scrappy street dogs. A few of the kids are gathering sticks and little rocks to throw, screeching with delight.

There's another dog who had been hoping to put *his* penis in the bitch in heat. And it's hot. The afternoon sun is just now relenting, casting huge palm tree shadows down the street, turning the trees themselves into gigantic, orangey-gold, jagged, hot-pepper lollipops.

The heat, along with the anguish of watching a stranger stretch out his lady crush, sweeps the spectator dog into madness. He leaps at the throat of his tormentor, who swings his leg up and around his embarrassed temptress, and now faces his opponent. His lady is now safe and out of the way, tucked behind him, his penis amazingly twisted 180 degrees out the back of his legs. A highly strategic move for a dog, I thought.

You probably have to be pretty crafty to survive these streets. I'd like to offer this *dick move* as proof.

Those kids right there could tell you all about that I bet, runnin' around with chipped up ears and big scabs. That's not too bad though, they look happy. Most of 'em still have a chance to grow up and lay bricks in the sun for $12 a day. For now, they are enraptured. Someone's ear is gonna get a piece chipped out of it.

Jealous, the determined mutt approaches. Unfettered with sanity or lodged accompaniment, it leaps at the Australian Shepherd mix who rears up, twisting in the air, and bites the attacking dog's neck. He then uses his shoulder and arm to deflect him, unbalanced to the ground. The challenger's feet slip like a bad ice skater, and he hits his head on the ground with an honor sacrificing *yelp!* The shepherd steps around, his honey reversing his every step, in perfect choreography with her stud.

The children go mad. They throw their sticks straight up in the air, then scramble for them so they can chase after and pelt the vanquished dog, who has retreated to his original spot where he first felt the hatred, hoping he had left some behind. It's a dry well, though. We find that out when he scurries down the street as half the kids run after him, throwing sticks and rocks, screeching, taunting, and howling.

I remember it being funny that his tail actually was between his legs. You always hear it but never see it. Half of the 3-7yo kids remain behind, semi-circling a spot near the gutter where the conjoined canines broil along with their schedule busting tragedy tryst.

Yesterday's flame has been vanquished to the cornfields. The Shepherd is looking like this happens every day. The girl dog of an undeterminable breed doesn't even look that distressed, not in the throes of passion or anything. The date is over. They're ass to ass, heads as far apart as possible. Are they fighting already? What? He didn't kick his ass good enough? His head touched dirt! He yelped! Of course, they might be staying in position in case the kids decide to try something. The urgency is gone, and the kids, having lost interest, begin diminishing as their shopping mothers come out and giggle at the dog predicament.

They collect their little street scrappers and delegate bundles of corn tortillas and bags of beans to them. I look again at the dogs, and the valiant Shepherd seems to feel me looking, suddenly turns his head to look at me, like, "Hey buddy, your five minutes is up, why don't you go in the fuckin' store? Me and my lady are doin' somethin' alright? We'll send you a fuckin' postcard from the honeymoon." I do that.

The whole scene just strikes me. I think maybe there is something to Prabhu's reincarnation philosophy because I swear that stuck dog is Bruce Lee. That arm move? The deflection that sent the other dog on his head? It was insane! I'm visualizing it in the store in slow motion and bump into somebody, *"Lo Siento, Señora."*

I'm to get poblanos, garlic, tomato sauce, cheese, and parsley. I quickly wrap up business and walk out of the store to find the dogs gone. Hopefully, disconnected, and overflowing with well-earned bliss.

Susan

One fine sunny morning, I visit the bridge that crosses the river
on Insurgentes Street, and my sister Hannah is up there selling
stingray *ceviche*. She is singing it for the whole block to hear, *"Ceviche!
Acapulco estilo!"* $2 for a 16-ounce Styrofoam container with a spork.
Everyone in the family has their hustle to get the pocket change we need
for *extracurriculars*.

Sadly, she doesn't sing much anymore now that she's a young adult. It
seems like just last week; she was still a kid playing with all her animals
at the teepee. Singing, dancing, and laughing. She's an Amazonian now.
Picture a barefoot, blonde, Viking, teenaged girl. She always wears her
trademark floor-length, flowy dresses, and she seems to be content to
just be, *no need to get anywhere, everything is fine.* A force of cheer and
calmness in a busy part of town.

And why not? Up here on top of the bridge is a rather lovely place to
perch. Looking down the river, there is a squadron of birds racing
towards us just an inch above the water, working in synchronicity that
dry feathers rely on. They pass right on under the bridge at Mach speed,

and now we're watching their backs fly away. They will be back in five minutes…and five minutes after that.

A line of Huichol Indians walks by in their impressively white cotton outfits, setting up blankets to sell their art on top of. They live out in the desert and search their souls under the starry night sky with the help of *peyote*. This results in some awesome art that makes Salvador Dali look sober and Pablo Picasso look like an amateur. I hear if they like you, they will take you out and get you high in their traditional homelands. The outskirts of which are just a car journey from town.

They will guide you through your trip. The Huicholes have to like you, though. You can't just go up and offer them money to do it. They'll get offended because *peyote* is sacred, and you can't exchange money for it. This tribe of Mexican desert Indians are world-class artists, and they've come to town to sell their masterpieces for a tenth of what they're worth. They will carve a piece of wood into a jaguar head and coat it with bee's wax, then stick colored beads into the wax. This leaves you with a bright, multi-colored jaguar head with a *peyote* button nose and a bird of phoenix on its forehead. They will sell you the finished work for $30. It probably took a guy two days to make it. It belongs in a museum. You should really give him at least $50, you stingy curmudgeon.

I watch people haggle these poor guys, and I want to just kick them a swift one to their asses. Guys will roll through and buy all their stuff in bulk so they can bring it back to America and charge $120 for that $30 piece. I consider managing the careers of these exploited, bead mosaic, master crafters.

After taking in the bridge life for a bit, I go down by the cheap restaurant that has the good tortillas, enough lard in the beans, spectacular chorizo, scrambled eggs, crema, and that crumbly white cheese I like. The hangover helper. This white girl, who is eating by herself, is watching me blow smoke rings with the cheap unfiltered cigarettes called Faros that cost you about 75-cents a pack. I had bought some last night when I was drunk, which is the only time I ever buy a pack. Gross. She doesn't know I know she's watching me, and I make a real show of it, presenting my Claudia Schiffer lips like it's a movie audition for a Weinstein flick.

Next thing you know, I'm at her table asking her if she knows where the post office is—I know where the post office is—Her name is Susan. She's pretty cute, chipmunk cheeks, big seductive lips, brown hair, and browner eyes. A big, round and joyous butt. She's 26, like me, and she lives in Portland. She is here on a girls' trip, but they're all off on a tour that she was too hungover for. Somewhere there is a donkey with no rider.

We hit it off, and she asks me if I want to go back to her room and take a nap. I take this to be code for a savage flesh romp and follow her up the stairs to her room, watching her ample, sweet ass swish and swash beneath her tiny waist. The bottom of her skirt flickering at a paradise just hidden. The wood-slatted stairs bow into a smile as they get to take the peek I'm just out of range for. It's what lies just out of view sometimes that pushes a man to madness; the faint whiff and the hint of a pristine pleasure mound. It's been a while since I had some tender touch, and now would be a great time to release havoc on her Cu Chi Tunnel with my blood burrito most foul.

Inside the room are only two beds and about four American girls' worth of junk strewn everywhere. Time is of the essence. The others will be back. I dust off my semi-effective five-minute plan to get her pants off, which uses every tactic but saying, "I have cancer." This desperate ploy *might* get you sex, but it's dry, sympathy pussy. Fuck that. I haven't had a piece since I got here. I need something so wet and savage we might just drown in a mixture of blood and cum, still frantically fucking, as our final nose bubbles bob up through the gelatinous, two-toned life juice.

Unfortunately, the bitch really meant a nap. I am literally staring at her sleep with a stuffed-up jizz-rod that feels like a shaken-up champagne bottle with the cork glued in. At first, I think this is part of some flirty little *waiting game*, but then she starts a cute, light snore. *Damn it!*

Eventually, she wakes up, we make out a little and go to a movie. Perhaps after the movie, I could buy her some aphrodisiacal tacos, and that would pass a threshold where she could possibly enjoy some sexual *carne asada* without feeling too whorish. *Jesus, I'm desperate. Please fuck me, Susan!*

I start drinking in excited anticipation of what might come soon—what *must* cum. This leads to me talking during the movie. Maybe a movie wasn't the best idea on a first date. It's subtitled, and I figure everyone is reading the words, so I'm just chattering away thinking nobody cares, like a hyper, drunk idiot that's trying to score. It's a terrible movie anyway. Well, someone **does** care, because about midway through, I hear someone behind me say in a Canadian accent, "Hey Bud, we're a tryyinnn tah see thuuuuh mooovie. Cuhn ya keep it doan, please?" Canadians. Too polite to fight with, but still annoying, am I right? They're everywhere in this town. How much vacation time are they getting up there?

After the movie, we go get some tacos from a crowded stand. You want the crowded stand being run by an older chubby lady who yells things at the customers, like, "Pay attention!" or "Get out of the way!" At a place like this, you know stuff like meat freshness and TLC are going to be on the level. Only tourists get *Montezuma's revenge* because they don't know which places to avoid. Hint: it's the places with no Mexicans eating there! And melted ice cubes—sometimes it's the melted ice cubes. Enjoy those *margarita* slushies! You're basically holding a cup full of cryogenically frozen sea monkeys in your hand. Enjoy your stay at Sandals Resorts, suckers.

These fuckin' tourists go straight from the airport to the hotel and swim in the pool all day, take a big air-conditioned bus to the top of a hill and get out for a few minutes, then they go back to Colorado and tell everyone what Mexico is like. It's like everywhere you've ever been, fuckface. The created journey Sandals Corp made for you. Stop trying to roll the *r*s when you order burritos, Jerry. No one believes you. Also, those tacos you're eating later were made with about as much thought as an American peace treaty.

The poor Mexicans that work at Sandals are not about to give you seasoned meat. Those people are miserable, and so are the tacos they cooked way earlier this morning, which are now crawling with microbes. Those little stomach gurglings you feel, Seattle Steve? Those are quickly going to turn into a fiesta in your butthole that will have you begging for death by sunset. Was the all-inclusive package worth it, Steve? Was it?

What I'm saying folks, is that you need to get off the tourist strips. And once you do, tacos in Mexico are **fucking amazing**! They don't even really have burritos, and the ones they do have are half the size of a San Francisco Mission District burrito. Down here, it's all about <u>Tacos! Tacos! Tacos!</u> I don't know what it is. The tortillas just came out of a masa presser 30 seconds ago? When you order, they take them and fry 'em up on a hot propane griddle with a good amount of oil until the edges are brown and crispy? Then they ladle on some perfectly seasoned meats. It's up to you to squirt lime onto it through a top layer of cilantro and onion. Absolute perfection! The freshness and simplicity is the crux of it all.

This lady has probably made over a million tacos on this street since she was her mom's assistant, and now she presents to you the most lovingly folded protein wallets of joy. At a buck a pop, it's not the cheapest dinner you can get because you need at least six of them. The tastiest, though. I order some carnitas, steak, *lengua* (cow tongue), and a calf brain. We sit down on a curb with our paper plates and our Jarrito's sodas. She takes a big bite of one, chews it, and says, "Crazy texture, which one is this?"

"You're eating a cow brain taco. Is it good?" I laugh.

"Are you serious? You're not serious!" She looks horrified and de-pinches the taco, letting it fall and unravel. She starts inspecting the filling that fell.

"Ha-ha! It's good, admit it. Here, I'll take a bite," I say, going nuts laughing.
She spits out most of it and starts to get up to leave. I grab her by the shoulder. "Look, I forgot which plate the brain one was on, I'm sorry. Come on, that was the only one, I promise."

She's a bartender, so she's not a total wuss. The booze industry hasn't had time to totally destroy her innocence, giving her a delicate balance of sweet and sour for now. She just says, "You're an asshole!" and picks off the cilantro and onion on the next one to make sure it's regular meat underneath.

After that, she starts giving me regular handjobs, but she won't let me visit the *dew drop inn*, on account of she's not sure if she's done with her ex. She thought she might come down to Mexico and sample some various cocks to make sure. Mine is so potentially addictive she doesn't know how to proceed. A short-lived craven life of lust and addiction…or the comfort of regularity and safety? Her cross in the road.

Carne Bala Torta

I go into a restaurant with taxidermied bullheads all over the faded red walls. I see a guy sitting at the bar that owes me $20 on some dirt weed. I remember every single person that owes me for weed over the last 15 years. He's one of them. Changing countries only changes the currency, not the amount owed. Dirt weed debt is like student debt to me, that shit never goes away. I won't ask your wife for it at your funeral, but everything short of that? Expect it. "Mikey! How you doing you old salty bastard? Long time no see."

I'm prepared for him to not be happy to see me because of the debt, but I'm hard up. He's going to have to fess up something. I'm here to eat and drink anyway even if I didn't see him, so we can ease into it. It's mostly just good to see a guy from the old hood.

Mikey, not to be confused with Mikey from Kronyx, is a funny fucker. I like him. A short old hippy guy with a bit of a biker edge. Harley Davidson shirts, turquoise rings, an asymmetrical grey beard…voice almost as gravelly as Lemmy Kilmister. He used to wear glasses, but he kept losing them or breaking them drunk. He gave up, and now he just squints at people if he even cares to know who he's talking to. Mikey has seen some shit, but he keeps it mostly funny and light. His confident, fairly upright posture tells me he's not too drunk yet—and possibly flush!

He was a roadie for some well-known classic rock bands. I think even earlier than that too, like, Johnny Cash and shit. He has a lot of backstage stories that'll leave you trippin': *That Stevie Nicks, once she blew out her nostrils with cocaine, it was the new roadie's job to blow the cocaine up her asshole with a straw. You know, so she could get high? You'd think that that's an awesome deal, right? 'Hey, I'm blowing coke up Stevie Nicks' ass.' Right? But after she taps you on the shoulder for the fourth time and you're trying to get your own party going, it gets old.*

I never hear him tell the same story twice. "No, Mikey, I did **not** know that Sade is a heroin addict who is so out of it she doesn't even know she's famous."

Mikey is glad to see me. "Whoa, hey, man! There's Santa Barbara all over this town," he says with a big smile. "Invadin' and shit. Come, pull up a stool. Bartender? A drink for my friend."

He's obviously been drinking for a bit and is in his *extremely good mood* phase. This should last another hour or so until he starts phase three, where he accuses everybody of doing all his drugs, then passing out in a chair. I'll be gone by then, set the timer for 59 minutes. "I'll have a Pacifico and a shot of Cazadores," I say.

Mike glances over, realizing I'm going to try and work his whole debt off right here and now.

$15 to go, Mikey. "Can I get a food menu, sir?" I ask the bartender, still lookin' right at Mikey when I say it.

The bartender motions up to a chalkboard. There are a few things on there, but I don't see the meatball sandwich type thing I just saw walk by me out of the kitchen. Been a long time since I've seen something like that.

"So, how long you been down here, Mike? I saw you around a lot, and you disappeared on me. I was worried. Not enough to check the morgue, but you know, you were my daytime pool buddy. I hate playing with people that suck, especially if they ain't funny. They got a table in here?" I look around the room for the old *slate slab*. No luck.

Mike looks vibrant as fuck compared to the old dude I knew back in Santa Barbara. The environs must suit him down here. Younger and healthier than when I last saw him for sure. Still pretty shitty, but considerably better. It seems like he wants to talk about it too, and I guess I *would* like to know his secret.

Here he goes: "I've been down here a year, ever since my Social Security kicked in. Been livin' like a king! The senoritas don't say I'm a dirty old man if I compliment them, food is good, sun is good, beer is cheap. Rent is $150. It's paradise. I feel young again!"

Mikey is going on a roll, "And get this, you heard about them new pecker pills on the market? The blue ones? Viagra? Oh man, I been drivin' these *senoritas* wild, man! Five years ago, *rigor mortis* wouldn't have stiffened my pecker. But now, all of a sudden, I'm making girls half my age cum their god damned brains out. They're following me around like little puppy dogs! It's fucking magic! Ah, my friend, life is an amazing thing, but you got to be able to **drink** hard, **eat** lard, *and* **get** hard! Without one, you fuck up the rhythm of life, brother."

We raise a toast to that, as Mikey finishes his story. "I only drink half what

I used to now because I'm not depressed anymore. The man you knew in Santa Barbara was a sad man. Now I'm a fuckin' drinkin' to remember, not to forget. *Salud!*"

In every third world country, you will, from 1998 on, find guys like this. Old, ugly white dudes, looking for a last chance at youth, and for a while, finding it. And now they will be armed with Viagra. No one is more underpaid than a third world hooker at the end of the 1990s, that's for fuckin' sure. Some of those hookers got rich, but at what cost? Bunch of retired white dudes with 16yo peckers running around suddenly? They ain't had a woody in 20 years, and now their *pussy poles* can stay hard as a diamond for four hours at a time? It turns them 16yo mentally too. Acting stupid, getting married after a week to a *gold digger*—in most cases, *copper digger*—jumping off a roof if the whore don't love 'im back. It's pathetic. Guys are getting dragged out of the hourly hotels to finish the last half of their heart attacks in the gutter—whores just paying themselves out of his pants, giving the overworked ambulance crew a chance to pick the rest.

I ponder the facets and implications of this new pharmaceutical development. It seems like a big mess to me. "Those poor whores, Mike. You at least let 'em turn the lights out, right?"

"Fuck a duck, cousin! You make a bitch cum five times in an hour? You look like motherfuckin' Jim Morrison to 'em. I tell one of 'em that I'm homeless, so the other chick that *knows* where I live don't kill her."

"Ha-ha. You always were a clever drunk, Mike. I'm glad you've found your paradise. I'm enjoying the hell out of this place, too, although all I'm getting so far is handjobs. What's the line on weed or pool hustles around here?" I look around to assess the possibilities. Looks shitty.

"Handjobs! That's bullshit. Handsome, charming piece of shit like you? In the sexual prime of his life? I don't believe it. I want a handjob from a stranger? I just crank it with the right hand. You want to fuck my third-stringer? She's a little bitey. She gets into it. A little *too* into it for me, personally. I'm old school, I don't go for all that butt stuff, scratching… extra gear. My cock, your pussy; that's all I want."

"I'll think about it, Mikey," I lie, trying to be as diplomatic as possible to get this debt whittled down to *nada*. It's always great if you can do that and not ever have to bring it up if it's someone you like. This dude is classic. I like him a lot.

Mikey gets to the storytelling part of his nightly drunk, "Did I ever tell you about the time I saw Janis Joplin piss standing up?"

"No, Mikey."

"She stood up and pulled down her pants and did some little finger trick, where she spread the top of her pussy out sideways, and she had this little pussy nozzle pointed straight out. She let a stream out thicker'n a Shetland Pony. Damn near put the fire out."

"That's crazy, Mikey. Just when I think you can't top the last story. Janis Joplin? For real?"

"It wasn't Joan of fuckin' Arc, kid."

I can't get that meatball sandwich out of my mind. I come up with the words in Spanish for meatball sandwich. I call the bartender over for another shot of tequila and to order said sandwich. The *mariachi* band that had been working its way around the restaurant in their silver buckles all down the pant leg, red bow ties and velvet sombreros, finish a song, but I'm still trying to talk over them. Way louder than necessary. "Can I have another Cazadores and a *carne* (meat) *bala* (ball) *torta* (sandwich)?"

The whole bar area erupts with hardcore laughter because they know what I'm trying to say, but what a ridiculous and hilarious way to get there. I guess it's like when you read a Chinese menu, and they try to explain something using English. *"Start to stop the keeping warm jar,"* *"Happy past life!"* This must have been better than that, though, because these people are going wild in here. Ex-pat Americans, Canadians, and Mexicans alike. I've got to remember this one. A stand-up comedian would be looking for a way to wrap it up at this point, knowing he can't top it. Mikey's face gets red, and he's cackling like a hyena on mushrooms. He's really going at it. Spit coming out down on his chin, the whole bit. I feel like he's going to break a hip falling off his fuckin' stool.

After eating my *albondigas*—Mexican meatballs—with toast and another round of drinks, I part ways with Mikey. He hands me a hundred peso note for interest. I probably look a little scrappier than usual, and he figures I need it. I'm glad he doesn't bust out coke. I think I'm strong enough to resist it, but who knows?

Truth be told, I could score cocaine down here if I really want to, so I'm doing good. Since I've been here, I never craved it. I really think it's Santa Barbara for me; everybody needs to leave their home town as an adult. The boredom sets in, dope seems fun, the nose candy is right there, being offered by a friendly and familiar face that knows you well and just what to say, "Just a key bump to get the night started. I only have a 20 bag anyway. Once that's gone, we won't score anymore."

Leave your hometown kids. Come back and retire if you really want, but see the world. Especially if you can't afford it. The resourcefulness will guide you to the light. I almost promise.

I get up to leave Mikey. Everyone has been patting me on the back for the biggest laugh they've had all week like I'm "Norm" from Cheers. I take the last look I'll ever take of Mike, sitting there on a bar stool, just like I always found him. I hit the sidewalk feeling happy. Good dude, that Mikey. Except for the marauding about with a perma-woody, terrorizing the poor overworked vaginas of any prostitute unfortunate enough to come within a car length—if he squints—peripheral view. *Run Maria! Run!*

Yelapa

Things are a bit rocky between Susan and me because she made out with this dude that I hate. I hate him because he's friends with Carlos, who had been partners with my brother out at the Krishna temple growing vegetables. They shared a plot there and sold them at a market. They had a falling out where Carlos headbutted my brother. She knew all about that too; disloyal, *dick stroke Madonna*.

I go tearing around town looking for Carlos, I find him in a bar, and he almost falls to his knees, kissing my ass trying to explain what happened. Not being in my element, I let him off the hook. I hear *gringo* life isn't that pleasant in the local lock-up. The cops don't have too much of a problem taking you there in cases of violence or property damage. I definitely don't have the bribe money that I would need to avoid that, or I would crack him in the jaw right here and now.

About a week later, Carlos' idiot friend Teo, the Mexican Sylvester Stallone, vibes me at the temple. Apparently, he saw Susan out at the bars...claims he made out with her. I start talking shit to him, calling him 'a liar,' and Prabhu Prakash gets upset. I tell Prabhu what Teo just said in my shittily attempted Spanish, and Prabhu admonishes Teo.

So now, both of these lops are on my shit list. Auggie and Carlos continue to have problems, and Carlos says he's called immigration on us. He thinks that deportation works both ways; that Mexico is deporting Americans left and right. Ha-ha. We laugh at him, and I plot to beat his ass the next time I see him off temple grounds. That other bitch Teo too. Buff guys are always confident until their nose is gushing blood onto their pretty muscles.

I go out to Yelapa with my sister, Hannah, to ask Susan if it's true what Teo said. She's been living out there for a week with her friends from Portland. Real homely types that like to remind me she *sort of* has a boyfriend.

She confirms that it's true, she made out with Teo. I should have known, the last handy she gave me was a bit passionless and ended with more of a *courtesy spurt* than an endorphin blast for the ages. Susan is crying. She says her boyfriend found out about the palm pussy I was scoring, and now he's flying down here in two days to rescue her from sin. I decide to let her go. After all, it's just handjobs. Sorry, you cried at the end, Susie baby.

I go down to the beach of Yelapa, determined not to let the trip out here be wasted. We had to take a boat to get here, after all. Yelapa is not an island; they just never wanted a road built here through the dense woods that surround the village, which runs along a little river through a low canyon that empties out into a beautiful blue bay. The sand is white with just enough warmth to lure you into a state of jellied relaxation without burning your toes. Beers are 2 whole bucks, which is disappointing. It's due to everything having to come in on the tiny boats. Fortunately, kids come around with cheap homemade liquor in hollowed-out gourds. It's called *ricea,* and it is as cheap as it is hammer hitting.

The people are unique products of only this place, and they want it to stay that way. They definitely have their own warm and welcoming character that is far different from what you get in Tijuana, which, as I previously mentioned, is what I thought all of Mexico was like before this. Yelapa is just a beautiful place on the planet. Don't go unless you're cool, ok? The villagers carry on with their lives and traditions almost as if you aren't here, inviting you to observe if you like, and possibly befriending you if you stick around.

One such occasion that I am able to watch them do something really cool is when I approach their soccer field. At one end, they have a 30-foot tall wooden pole staked into the ground. It's entirely greased in pig lard. The kids of the village form a human pyramid to the top, which holds a bag full of tequila, candy, soap, corn nuts, and other assorted loot. The pyramid is almost there! The smallest kid in the village clambers up everybody's backs all the way up there and snatches it, raising it in victory before he scrambles back down the triangular flesh tower. The crowd goes wild! Everybody laughs and smiles as the kids divide up the goods.

The difficulty of getting to Yelapa in a tiny overloaded boat prevents most of the resort clingers from coming here. That is fine with the Yelapans. They have a small but steady flow of backpackers and hardier travelers that come here to eat from the row of seafood taco stands on the beach. There is no better place to be than under a *palapa* in Yelapa. There are a few more things to do: take a donkey ride back to the waterfall along the river lined with everything from huts to fancy houses. There's a discotheque on Fridays—that's today!

I'm dancing there with this girl I spotted earlier in the day, Lorena, of Mexico City, a hot, **hot** *Chilanga*. She's pretty, tall, with a sharp, long nose, giving her a semi-birdlike face. She has beautiful green eyes and long sexy legs, which you can see all of in her short, fray edged denim shorts. Her smile more than intrigues me. My sister, over 18 now, is legally allowed to drink. She laughs when I motion to the beauty and says it looks like a Mexican version of my first girlfriend, Shawna. I guess it's true. A happy accident? Or maybe I really do have a type. Long pretty legs with a bird face?

I leave her at the table with a beer and some *flautas*. Lorena and I dance, locking eyes before she tries to flit away from me, smiling, egging me on to follow. We dance for a long time to ABBA and worse. It could have been a hobo grinding his dentures into the loudspeaker while a bunch of screech monkeys belted out their version of "Danny Boy." My flip flops and I would still be dancing on air, sliding like James Brown across the sand granules, into a spin or a leaned back sex pose, which only fully extends the second before the song, "I'm Too Sexy," ends. I see it in her eyes the second she decides I'm going to visit the *pink palace*. Handjob time is over. Time for the adults to play.

We sit and have a few drinks and socialize with some other Mexicans. The kid that is angling for a job to translate for us is back with the condoms I ordered, except it's only one! I give him 50-pesos anyway, as a retainer to stick around. This girl speaks zero words of English. *More to come, kid.* We go to leave, and I don't see Hannah. What?! I look around outside the bar, go back and look inside. Nothing. I figure she wouldn't have left if she didn't have a place to stay. I know she has been here a few times before and knows people. A boyfriend? Nah. I'll find her on the beach tomorrow.

We arrive at Lorena's rental house. It overhangs the beach, more of a lanai with a bathroom. There's only a rail dividing us from the waves, which splash on the rocks just below. Lorena tells me, in a slow Spanish, that I can understand, that she has a boyfriend named Oscar in Mexico City. When she comes to the coast, she forgets about him.

Why you telling me his name, sweetheart? I guess in Mexico I'm Mr. Backdoor Man. Not a role I have ever felt good about, but I'm not in the position for sexual morality right now. I'm two steps away from fucking a rolled-up, soapy sock.

We fuck sweetly, then hard. Lorena arches her back until I can count the ribs. She cums on top of me. Now it's time to pound it from behind. The tip of my cock catches on an interior ledge of her pussy walls, the first quarter inch of her flips inside out like a shiny, purple, O-ring sweatband on the head of my angry John McEnroe. My cock rams in and out, popping out like a cork each time. I repeatedly flick-flack the interior pussy ridge with the edge of my rock-hard Wimbledon master. The fast, hard rhythm and the *pop popping* of my dick tip starts the countdown until I explode. Months of waiting for a decent payoff ends now.

Shuttle thrusters begin to engage in my balls. Everything from my dick tip, through the taint, to the center of my asshole begins to quiver and vibrate. An intense tingling, repeated contractions of ecstasy, growing stronger and closer with each repetition until my frontal lobe throbs in ticklish, electric unison with my cock and balls. *"Uuunnngghhh!!!"* I cut the boosters loose. About 2-ounces of it. My crescendo starts her on another round of orgasms, so I pump and pump before the part of my dick that controls hardness figures out that I jettisoned the payload.

I grab her hair and twist it to push her over the edge. I get up from my knees, and in a ruthless squat of direct penetration, I lean back on my heels. This uses gravity and leverage to launch her pussy down onto my determined, *overtime worker* of a dick.

"Aaaaahhhhhhhhh! Dios!!!!!!," she screams before collapsing in a shudder. *Adios* is right…to my overheated, quivering fuck stick. I fall to the sheets, and we sleep the deep sleep of the sexually satisfied as the ocean waves break next to us.

The next morning, we go to the beach to eat, and wouldn't you know it, there's Susan and her friends. Team Homely eye rolls me as Susan looks at the ground, obviously mad. They don't like it when you move on quickly. I'm not happy to rub it in even though I'm pissed that it was Teo she made out with. That anger went away when my blue balls did. Let's call it even.

Am I supposed to feel bad that I was able to hopscotch down the *candy highway* so quickly? It was dumb luck. Plus, there are only three places that serve *chorizo* and eggs around here, and they're all lined up next to each other on the beach. All 25 gringos in town are pretty much here right now. It seems like Susan has a pretty complicated social life right now, so I'm perfectly happy to simplify it by bowing out. Peace? She still looks pissed. Whatever.

I look towards the beach to detoxify from her vibe, and I see a guy getting a *Yelapan alarm clock*: when a tourist avoids a lodging fee by just sleeping on the beach, drunk. The local kids come and cover your back with stale *tortilla* chips, and you wake up to 50 seagulls pecking at you. Pretty funny, actually. Soon, my sister arrives. "Uh, I passed out in the bar, and some lady was nice enough to rescue me. Thanks a lot."

"What?!" I'm horrified. "How did you pass out on beers? Are you ok?"

"I drank some of that *ricea* stuff. The boys were just giving it to me free."

"Oh, no. I got…distracted," I say guiltily.

"I can see that." She looks at Lorena, who senses the conversation has taken a dramatic tone. I reassure her, it's just my sister, and she relaxes. The weird *other girl* energy must be coming from somewhere around here, she seems to be thinking. Not that she acts jealous; girls just pick up on that.

I have failed my sister the first time I ever even drank with her. Maybe we should have brought mom. I have never been the greatest big brother, and it looks like that's not going to change. I feel a little of my sex buzz die down as some shame dilutes it.

In the afternoon, Lorena hops on a little boat. "She writes her phone number in Mexico City down in dainty little numbers and letters to create an illusion that we'll meet again someday. This allows a hopeful whim to hang in the air as we kiss one last time. I hold her hand as she steps into the boat and watch her bounce over the little waves, out of the azure bay. I never see her again. It's a honey tinted picture that is a perfect ending to a lovely, short-lived liaison. Thank you, Lorena. I hope you have a joyous life. Hannah and I hop a boat later in the afternoon, leaving behind my best Yelapa experience; and Hannah's worst.

Headed Back North

I leave a week later. My screenplay is finished. The crucial puzzle piece in finding some purpose and constructive activity to give my life meaning. I can't just keep moving back to Santa Barbara every time shit doesn't work out. It can't be the places—I've tried several—it must be this inner turbulence I have to get a hold on. I read my script and think out long philosophical equations such as this as the hot Sonoran Desert sun beats down on the long road, which stretches out like a big piece of melted black licorice.

The second night on the bus, I have a dream that I'm awake at night on the bus, and I look out the window, and Kit is out there, not running but keeping up with the bus. In the dream, I yell, "Driver stop the bus!" He does and lets me off and drives away. I run up to Kit and say, "Kit? I thought you were dead." Kit just stands there smiling at me and shaking his head, *No* and somehow, I know that he's not shaking his head, *No, I'm not dead*. He's shaking it, No, we don't need to talk. So, we don't. I just stand there looking at him, and he's so real looking, and I'm overcome by sadness and happiness at the same time. He's smiling that magic smile of his, and it is charging me like a battery.

I wake up in my bus seat and desperately look out the window for Kit, but he's not there. I think Kit really was out there in the Sonoran Desert that night. It's hard to explain. I think he wanted to tell me he was proud of me for writing the screenplay and to keep my chin up. I guess I'm saying that I believe spirits can visit you in your dreams. I wrote it, Kitster!

Eventually, I get back to Tijuana, cross over, and ride the Amtrak from San Diego to Santa Barbara. This gorgeous curly brown-haired woman named Tracy is talking to me. She's really into my purple and brown peasant clothes that my mom sewed for me. Tracy is 40ish and looking very good. I tell her some stories about my travels. She tells me about the Columbine High School shootings that just happened, and we agree that that is a crazy fluke.

"Who shoots up a school? Nothing like that would ever happen again, for sure. There's definitely a problem at schools with bullies, and now that this has happened, they'll have to fix it, right?" I say.

I'm being agreeable, and who am I to shatter her optimism? Flirting with strangers on a train is all about *escapism*. Dodge those serious conversations and just let fantasy flourish, man. If the world burned around us as we fuck, I'd whisper to her, "That's just friction, baby. That's not fire. Don't worry, everything is going to be fine. Close your eyes, and twist your ankles behind your head. Let me sip your juice box. The world isn't ending at all."

The taste of sex Lorena had given me was terrific, but it has also awoken the beast—a beast that must be fed. Tracy gets off in LA and hints that I should come with her. Everything short of the double entendre, "Do you want to get **off**?" I'm down to my last $20, and I'm not sure how I would get home if she didn't give me money in the morning. I would be a prostitute to bring this up in blunt terms at the moment, and with the train rolling to a stop for only three minutes, I don't have time for anything else. LA is a vast jungle, especially to the broke and unconnected. I wuss out and instantly regret it as we start rolling away. I can't stop thinking about it, and I have a woody sticking through my thin peasant pants now.

After an hour, I'm still getting intermittent wood thinking about it, and I decide to just go jack off in the bathroom to be done with it. So, there I am, jacking my peen, ashamed but determined. I just take the short route to the quickest orgasm that starts with her ample cleavage and quickly leads to a flip over to doggy style. The cleavage is so recent I don't have to use anything from my *mental file for jacking it on the go.*

When you grow up as a homeless teenager, you learn to just jack it when no one is looking—what I'm saying is, I've cranked jizz onto a tree. Soon, my balls quickly join the rumbling of the train cars, and I spew onto a wad of toilet paper. *What?! There's blood in my sperm!* I go back to my seat, hands snapping into their familiar tremble for the first time in a while. *What the fuck? I didn't use a rubber the second time on Lorena because the kid only brought me back one. Fuck! Could my most fondly remembered lay in years have been contaminated? What in the Mexico City is this shit? Blood sperm?* The rest of the ride is a rather worry-filled affair, to say the least.

After I get off the train in my nemesis city, Santa Barbara, I walk into the hospital and just approach the first doctorly type with a silver beard that I see. "Doc? I have blood in my sperm. Should I go to the emergency room?"

He assures me it's probably just a minor prostate infection and not to worry, it'll work itself out. Shit. That's a relief. I've *raw dogged* a lot of girls, and I figured I was bulletproof at this point. My youthful stupidity had me rolling into battle like Sitting Bull, riding out into the bullets with my eyes closed, arms spread to the heavens, never getting touched. Something was bound to happen with *that* attitude. Thank god, or whatever is in charge of that. I swear I will never *free-blast* the insides of a hot Chilanga again if this clears up like the doc says. I'm a changed man. I have a purpose now.

I don't feel like settling back into this town of my perpetual vice. For a few days, I just walk around town wrapped in a brown horsehair blanket Prabhu Prakash gave me. I want everybody to think I went crazy down there just to mess with them. I tell them about the Temple, the ghost visitations in the Sonoran Desert, popping chickens, and everybody goes, "Yep ... J.C. is crazy! That boy really lost his mind this time!" After a bit of this, I realize I can't come back here again, so I move to San Francisco with $50.

The Mission District

I arrive with my usual duffel bag full of clothes, except something is different this time. They are actually cleaned and folded. And I have a major purpose to accomplish. To make a movie! I've got the screenplay, now all I need is some money, and nobody is going to stop me from getting it. That's why people move to the big city right to get money? Now just point me in the direction where the biggest concentration of it is so I can get on with my life, will you?

I take up lodging behind Walgreen's on Capp Street, close to 16th, at you guessed it, Motormouth Scotty's house. It's been a year since we had to break up the band. He's since relocated to San Francisco, The City by the Bay. Pot Plant Sarah is up here too, going to culinary school to be a chef. So, you know, I'm not exactly starting from scratch. I figure two weeks on each of their couches, and by then, I should have a paycheck from somewhere.

I look around and see that this particular neighborhood hasn't changed much since I got run over by a cop car here a dozen years ago. Junky shit on the sidewalk, $20 hookers everywhere, and from the looks of them, that price is a little high.

Everybody yells out to you as you pass, trying to sell you dope. I think the schools should bring kids on field trips down here and say, "Ok, kids. This is how cool crack and heroin is. When you do crack and heroin, this is where you have to hang out all day, and all night too, because even if junkies could sleep, they'd have nowhere to do it!" If you show a kid this shit, he'll never do drugs if he has any brains.

These, *"one and ones!"* are still the big seller on 16th and Mission—two tiny balloons; one stuffed with a little heroin, the other cocaine—You can get anything else you need out here too, provided it's illegal and poisonous for you. Crooked syringes and broken crack pipes conceal themselves amongst trash piles, hoping to latch onto a careless pedestrian so they can pollinate abroad.

They send poor people, whose shady side-hustle became known to the cops, to do community service here. They sport bright reflector vests to clean the gutters and sidewalks of <u>District, One and One</u>. They only move the trash from one part of the gutter to another with their brooms. They stop to check the crack pipes for any leftover residues or to find a reasonable price on heroin from a passing dealer familiar to them. The dealers blatantly transact in front of cops that prefer to spend their time on more important matters, such as 'second lunch break.'

Mission Street makes Tijuana look like Laguna Beach. Just a block over, on Valencia Street, a major revamp is underway, a complete remake from its former grittiness. It's actually now safe at night—kind of. The microcosms of San Francisco can be quite amazing to behold. On this block, you can get stabbed with a dirty needle for not giving a junky a dollar, but you go over 50-yards that away? Bill Gates is signing autographs at a fucking sushi gala.

There is a technology boom happening in 1999, and the bubble hasn't popped yet. You can come up with the stupidest shit ever to put on a billboard, and as long as there's a **.com** at the end of it, the venture capitalists will pour buckets of $100 bills over your head. Silicon Valley has suddenly been packed full of millionaires, and they are now spilling into the Mission District as if from a giant shit bag with a hole popped into the side of it.

Couch Surfin' USA

I resolve to find a new crash pad as soon as possible, but it would be a long month before I can get beyond the degradation of Capp Street. It's the alley that runs behind Mission Street. It exists mostly for deeds too dirty to be committed on Mission Street itself, which is really saying something. I am living in Motormouth Scotty's living room with two pit-bulls and a wolf.

They don't particularly care for the fact that I have shown up and taken over the couch. I know that they used to spend a lot of time on there because I wake up every morning to a mouthful of dog hair. Billy and Ella, the pit-bulls, start licking my face around sunrise to let me know my six-hour couch shift is over. Luna, Scott's white wolf, is chill and likes having me here. She has watched me, and Scott do a lot of drugs together without judging us too harshly. Beautiful dog. An agent of tranquility.

I get up and sneak in the shower before the morning bathroom traffic jam begins. Also, to be out before the warehouse owner's wife sees me and gives me the look of, "Oh, you're going to be here a third week?"

Her husband, Brett, is a cool lanky dude that I know from the old days of Isla Vista. He used to go to his classes naked and high on LSD. Anything that freaks out campus is cool with me.

If it weren't for his new wife, I would be living up in this bitch with my own room. She knows I'm using this place to start from scratch. I'm always the first friend the new wives get rid of, and I'm getting less and less subtle hints as the days, all too quickly, go by. *I'm trying my best to get out of your hair. Trust me. Do you know how hard it is to get a job when your sleeve is covered in dog hair? And there's no decent deodorant to steal some swipes off of in the bathroom because everybody that lives in this warehouse is a Grateful Dead enthusiast. I'm trying to use armpit crystals for hygiene. It's bullshit!*

Employers love seeing "couch surfer" written across your forehead. Then they can offer you the dishwasher job. Fuck that. I'm trying to bartend with my lie of a resume. I get canned after a week at Pier 23 because, among other things, I put Kahlua in an Irish Coffee. I bust my ass in that joint for nothing. The $200 check from there comes just in the nick of time, but The City pretty much just says, "Yeah, I'll be needing that. Thanks, sucker!" The City's ruthless, sisters and bros.

The only thing cheap is burritos around here, so at least there's that. Even though I'm usually sneaking on the bus, I'm spending about $20 on every afternoon job search. Do the bosses think I'm a country bumpkin or something? This is the only area of life I have never been confident in, and it shows. Cell phones are still a newish thing, so they're expensive as fuck. I can only afford a message service, so if people call me, I can't pick up the phone and answer. I get paranoid that people are getting the message center and hanging up. My one good job-hunting outfit is getting shabby looking. I'm running out of time.

Scott saves me in that respect because his high school friend, a suit store manager, needs some good looking kids to be in the store's local TV commercial. Scott volunteers himself, Pot Plant Sarah, and me.—Sarah is in Cordon Bleu chef school, and she's killing it. If there's a woman who can break into the male-dominated world of chefery, it's her.

We shoot the commercial in an afternoon in a San Jose park. It's a romantic ditty where Sarah is in love with the store manager. Scott and I are there to do some sizzling catwalks that make no sense to the story. We are all dressed in Italian silk suits and Vera Wang for Sarah. There's a limo in the commercial that we are filmed partying in. Perhaps we're supposed to be celebrating the stock market hitting a record high just as our technology start-up reaches public offering. "Yay! Pop the Bubbles Motor Mouth!"

"Ok, J.C.! *Pop!*"

"Are you going to make out with that guy Pot Plant Sarah? Because I wouldn't."

In the end, I come up with a way to just take the $800 suit, including the $300 Bruno Magli shoes, instead of the $300 cash payment. "Look, I accidentally scuffed the shoe. I guess you weren't going to sell all this stuff after we wore them all day, right?" I feel like I could get a job as a CEO wearing this thing! At the very least, it will help my confidence and eliminate the shabby outfit I've been rejected by half The City in. I could probably even go back to some of the old places, and they wouldn't even recognize me in this.

The guy goes for it, and Scott and Sarah get their outfits too. And get this, the guy lets us have the limo all the way back to San Francisco.

And it's loaded with booze! We go to the Up and Down Club on Folsom, go *up* and get some girls and bring them *down* into the double-parked limo to polish off the rest of the cognac. We let the limo go and go dance in our new suits. I feel like a king for the first time in a month since I made Lorena's brain melt in Mexico.

I hear the guy gets fired. We feel bad that it might have been for giving us all the clothes. The commercial runs in San Jose for a few years. Sometimes a techie will look at me with their head cocked, and I figure it's because of the commercial.

The *real* reason he probably got fired is that the technology bubble burst a bit later and dripped its goo all the way from San Francisco to San Jose, filling the nostrils and lungs of every dot com like some sort of *monkey virus*. Money might trickle down to the poor slowly, but the lack of it sure doesn't. Every waiter and bartender in San Francisco's tips got cut in half the day *that* was on the cover of *The Chronicle*. Great time to be trying to get established in the *tip getting* business. *Fuck!*

The techies—who had almost completed their hostile takeover of the entire city—were destroyed. Apparently, investing 100 million dollars in a sneeze medication site is risky. The City would be safe from their hostile takeover for now. They leave behind nothing but high rent and address sized husks, in exchange for the history they paved over. Phenomenal dive bars, that were really more like anthropological museums, replaced with idiotic, dorm-sized lofts.

"We'll be back," the Start-up Stuarts and Stanleys will say. And they will. It won't take long. When it all goes to shit—incredibly, in our near future—they'll have burnt their lips on that Nasdaq crack pipe, and they're gonna need a ride to rehab.

Never Get Surgery at a School

My wisdom teeth start challenging some of my molars around this time, and the pre-dawn root brawls get too much to bear. I don't have much money yet, so someone suggests I get it done at a dental school. People? **Don't get surgery at a school!**

Soon, I'm at the school, getting the surgery. The little lady that's showing the students how to get a wisdom tooth out is having trouble getting the bottom right tooth to surrender from its socket. This lady is climbing up on my chest, trying to get this thing loose, apologizing to the students watching that, "It's probably just the angle."

Hey lady, don't apologize to them. I'm the one being victimized here. She's taking it personally now like the tooth did something to *her*. She's ripping up the inside of my cheek and getting animalistic. I just want to get up and walk out, but then her supervisor looks in and says, "Judith? It looks like the patient is in some pain. Why don't we give him some more gas?"

"He didn't want any gas. He's just on Novocaine," Judith says.

"What?!" I try to say. "I wanted the gas! You didn't mention the extra $80 for gas on the phone! What the hell are you telling him I don't want the gas for? Bill me for the goddamned gas!"

Of course, I gather from the smiling students that I look as silly as I sound trying to mumble this through a jaw full of Novocain and blood. My ivory babes have been freshly torn from their little gummy arms, crimson spit dripping all over my paper bib, and my eyes are bulging out. Luckily for me, the head honcho is a large man, and he manages to uproot the tenacious devil fang. I'm sent home with a Codeine prescription and a dental X-ray that shows a polyp in my sinuses. I must have gotten that from my nights at the Mad Cat. I swear I'll never do a line of coke again. What a waste of a year—was it two? And now there's a cyst next to my brain? I *am* happy to report I'm doing well these days. Scott and I have only been boozing it up, and we've done X just a few times. I'm feeling healthy and mostly positive.

On the way, I decided to bring some flowers to Motor Mouth. I'd been really mean to him because when I showed him the script I wrote in Mexico, he said it needs a lot of work. I think the word "trite" was also used.

I'm getting him flowers because I found out he's in the hospital with this gnarly disease, *osteomyelitis*. I look it up and this is some nasty shit. It gets in your heart. You get a tube run through an artery straight into your aorta. A disease pretty much only heroin addicts get. What the fuck, Motor Mouth? I'll chalk it up to him living in the middle of Junky Town, and maybe something just blew onto his lip outside his house or something. Or he kicked a needle in his hippy Tevas.

As hard as we ever partied together, needles never came into the situation.

I have shot up a handful of times, mostly to see why my friends thought it was cool enough to die for. I wanted to see if I could understand the mechanics of the addiction, try to figure out a way to reverse engineer them out of it. I didn't see the attraction. It made me puke and get sleepy. I think it's only alluring to people in a lot of pain that would instead feel like they are in a drowsy embryonic jacuzzi sac. A chance to start over as a fresh baby perhaps.

On my way, through the 16th and Mission intersection, I see Scott on his way home from the hospital, and he's being helped along by his fiancé, Erin, a pretty young doctor, petite, short brown hair, and a perfect little button nose. I started dating a lawyer, so this asshole has to *high-hat* me and get engaged to a doctor he met at a rave. Whatever dude.

At any rate, Motor Mouth is making his way past the dirtiest Burger King in both hemispheres, and because he's very ill, accidentally bumps into this broke down pimp lookin' motherfucker. The guy looks rough. Like his hos ran away, and he's been brooding ever since. He's not exactly small either. He turns around and lifts his cane up, threatening to nail Scotty with it and says, "What's yo fuckin' problem white boy?!"

I'm right there within seconds, coming in from the side, and just before he drops the cane on poor Motor Mouth Scotty's head? I grab that shit and shove it back into his chest. He takes a step back, and I scream, "That's my friend, motherfucker!!! You better back the fuck off!!!!" but when I say it, it's through two rolls of gauze that are shoved into and around my three empty wisdom tooth sockets. I sound like a methed-up caveman from a haunted swamp. I hear that when I get pissed and start yelling my face turns purple and red, the veins start popping out all over, along with my bulging hateful eyes. I've probably gotten out of a few fights I might have lost because this blood vessel bluff worked and made them back down.

Brokey the Pimp takes one look at my insane mumble screaming ass and smartly shuffles off, talking some shit about, "Crazy white motherfuckers fuckin' up the neighborhood." *Yeah, buddy, because 16th and Mission was such a classy place **before** we got here.*

Needless to say, that fixes up me and Motor Mouth Scotty's relationship, and we go on to have a lot more unnecessary parties between us.

Scotty was right about my script anyway. My first foray sucked. Everybody's first script sucks, you're just amazed and impressed you're actually writing. The idea that you may be writing something amazing keeps your fingers tapping hard and your heart beating harder. Are you kidding? Even Les Claypool sucked in his first band, maybe. Fuck it, in the beginning, all you should care about is that you're playing, and that's more than most of the critics have ever done. Just keep going. It will be several thousand more hours of doing this shit before I consistently write something worth watching, reading, or listening to. So, thanks for being honest, I guess, Motor Mouth. Maybe don't use the word "trite" next time. I'd rather be a stupid bitch than an unoriginal bitch. Lack of originality was never anything anyone has credibly accused me of anyway.

Rat Race

Finally, I get a break from a catering company, and they send me to rich people's houses, where I witness portraits of excess that I thought only existed in Hollywood movies. There's a guy dressed in a tuxedo, and his only job is to cut smoked salmon with a big old knife and balance it on toast with some capers and dill crème fraiche.

On the balcony is the bar I've set up. A lot of the guests will tip me $20 and have me ruin $30 a shot tequila with 50-cent sweet and sour. The host usually gives me at least $100 and a bottle of wine at the end of the night. All this in addition to the $15 an hour I'm getting from the catering company. I haven't made this kind of money and not put it right back up my nose in a long time. Amazing. Finally, some hard work is paying off. Slowly but surely.

I justify my partnership with them by thinking, *Ah, rich people aren't so bad. Pitiable, but certainly not the demons of my youthful anarchistic fantasies.*

Eventually, I get to work at some of the biggest places, but I never really manage to find a home. Something always happens. A bike-riding injury on my way to the restaurant, a cocksucker with seniority takes a disliking to me. Something about my face seems to make managers drool for discipline. Is it the permanent skater smirk? My aristocratic Anglo-Saxon features, which make the whip cracker excited he's lashing someone possibly above his station? Who knows?

I *do* wear my emotions on my sleeve and a chip on my shoulder. Maybe that's it—*Ding! Ding! Ding!* I can never get excited about a restaurant job, and I drink too much during shifts bartending the dive bars to make it too far. The register is always off somehow by $50 in either direction. I do succeed in putting down roots, however, and avoid having to go back to my abusive relationship with Santa Barbara. And that is all that matters.

The Old Man

Now that I'm *above board* and becoming legit, I decide to give my old Dad a call. Maybe I'll try to even get along with him. We haven't spoken for over ten years. I stand there at the phone booth for a while, trying to punch in the numbers. I do, and soon we start hanging out. He's a grandfather now, so he's a little softer than he was. My grandparents are coming down for Thanksgiving, so I'm supposed to show up. The bait is that they are going to give me a trust fund that's been waiting for me. A trust fund? That's right. There was a trust fund mentioned once before, but I had forgotten. Now, since I've been working for my own money for a while, had built some pride over it, I wasn't quite sure how I felt about accepting it. But soon, I decide that this is the universe's way of saying, *"Go ahead, make the movie."*

I agree to take the money but to feed homeless people with a part of it. After all, I have to clean up my karma from that year of coke dealing. Two? I think it was two. I figure that since my grandparents are wealthy, the trust fund is going to come out to at least $50,000. I decide that will be the perfect amount to make my movie since I've sworn to only make low-budget films to contrast the vanity, excess, and gluttony of Hollywood.

That's why I have chosen to make movies, to combat the vain, empty violence Hollywood shits into the minds of the world's youth every block-buster season. The Blair Witch Project came out this year, shot on digital video. It made millions and cost like $8,000 to make. Let's go that route. Finally, a technological innovation I give a fuck about. Digital video. Awesome.

So, Thanksgiving, the big trust fund, and the estranged side of my family. I feel awkward at times during dinner, like everyone is waiting for me to spill the beans on what I've been doing the past ten years. I don't want to make up some big story, but I don't want to tell them the truth either. All in all, it's a very pleasant experience. A man needs to feel a connection with his family. I learn I'm an uncle and that everyone is alive and happy. They're catching me at an all-time high, so it's unanimous. We're all still Scales-winners. I don't even tell them it ever wasn't that way. I just try to stick to the recent past, and I think they sense a large hole in the story, but I don't get *pigeon-holed*. The stuffing is excellent. Everything is wonderful.

After dinner, Grandma takes me aside and says with a serious tone, "You know, we put some money away for you for when you grew up."

"Yes, Grandma."

"You're going to save it, right? And not waste it?"

"Yes, Grandma."

Then she gives me the trust fund. It's $500. I had to try hard not to laugh because it's so comical. I already made phone calls and started spending this money, and it turns out to be $500. I hug her and say, "Thanks," and promise again not to waste it while my grandfather looks on approvingly.

Getting There Slowly

I'm jobless again because I was "allegedly" scheduled to bartend a private party when I was down getting my huge trust fund. Oops. It's hard to keep up with work-life when you're still half homeless. I am sleeping at Pot Plant Sarah's place, the old Jefferson Airplane house 10-yards off of Haight and Ashbury. My time ran out at Scott's house, and Sarah is my only friend in San Francisco that's close enough to be a temporary burden on.

We've all been sitting in there in the evenings together, drinking beer, listening to Motown with sprinkles of Jamiroquai, Foo Fighters, Beck, and, of course, Ween.

I've been sleeping inside, but Sarah's relationship with her classmate at culinary school is getting serious. The guy is coming over every night at this point. Prachon, a nice Thai dude whose Dad is friends with the King of Thailand, is just stomping my couch game. He should just give me the keys to his house. Shit dude. I don't think he realizes I'm the one sleeping on the sidewalk outside when he leaves in the morning. He's too sweet to try and get rid of. So, here I am, out in front of the house, wrapped up like a Yeti-sized burrito in the brown horsehair blanket that Prabhu Prakash gave me. *"Just another homeless hippy crashing out in the Haight, don't mind me."*

This goes on for a bit until I meet Itza. I'm working the door at a gay bar in the Castro. I was really facing having to move back to Santa Barbara if a job didn't turn up quick, so I put on my short shorts and pranced up into the gay district. Ok, there weren't any short shorts, but I smiled real big. And I didn't bother trying to bullshit together another resume.

Suddenly, I'm working an entry-level job as the door guy at a Republican gay bar called the Midnight Sun. It's technically known as a "video bar": music videos, Kids in the Hall skits, Wizard of Oz scene excerpts, Golden Girls one-liners, gay soft porn. All in these rapid-fire snippets that give you attention deficit disorder—excellent training for the I-phones to come.

The music videos usually suck. For five happy hours a week, I'm subjected to Cher, Madonna, Mariah Carey, Ricky Martin, horrible techno, Janet Jackson, and obligatorily, on the hour every hour, that fucking "Groove is in the Heart" song. It's like they have a week's worth of four-hour loops of this shit, and they're just hoping the cheap booze gets everyone drunk enough not to notice or care that they've heard it a bazillion times. Now, I love me some gays—they remind me of the Jews, persecuted and witty—but their music is absolute trash, generally speaking.

The Castro is San Francisco's Disneyland, Mecca, primary gay district. There is a Mad Maxy, satellite district called "South Market," a mile or two away. That's where the bears hang out. The delicate queens of the Castro are often scared of the bears with all their leather and unsafe, brutal, alley sex. The queens have turned their neighborhood into a bright, *foofy* contrast of that. A cotton candy celebration of mainstream gay culture to counterbalance the underground roughness of the bears. Glitter and Spice Girls everywhere.

In a surprise twist which bucks the neighborhood norms, the Midnight Sun's clientele and employees are mostly motherfucking George Bush fans, if you can believe that. Motherfucking gay Republicans. No shit. What the fuck, right? They have a shit ton of money and hate paying taxes. They are in gay Shangri-La, a protected bubble. They got theirs, so fuck the social issues. Fuck everybody but their bank accounts. I overhear some guys talking about how awesome it would be to have a second George Bush as president. 20 minutes later, I have to tell them to stop sucking each other's dicks by the urinal.

This experience solidifies my belief that it's not the colors of our skins that divide us so much, it's the content of our bank accounts. Here, you have some of the most persecuted people on the planet, as a group, and you take them out of that situation and give them a little money and privilege? Most of them turn into the blood-sucking, entitled oppressors they hated in a heartbeat. Fuck being a millionaire. Once you're a millionaire, you usually forget if you're gay, black, or scoliotic. You just think of yourself as rich, and everyone else is just shit on your shoe.

Bizarre world, man. Not the most awesome gig. I hate helping Republicans in any way, but this place allows me to finalize my toehold in The City. "Get money or go home!" the urban jungle screams at me as I struggle.

One day, I'm checking IDs, and a beautiful girl named Itza rolls through. Tall and skinny with tiny teeth inside a perfect lipped smile. Her face is basically the Nefertiti statue come to life. Just beautiful. She looks Ethiopian or Egyptian, but she's second-generation Panamanian. The only way she isn't skinny is those robust hips that bookend the most perfect ass I have ever seen. If I could touch that ass just once, I know it would imbue me with an inconceivable power that I'm not sure I would be able to avoid abusing. As Gollum had his soul polluting ring of invisibility, I have this *perfect* Nefertiti ass before me now. Tempting me, driving me slowly mad with lust. Jesus, look at it.

After she sucks down a few Cape Cods, I see her looking for our barely used women's restroom. I say, "Itza, the bathroom is over there." I remember her name because it's as uncommon as her beauty. She comes out and says, "Thanks." She is impressed that I remembered her name. Lock on the tractor beams!

We go on a couple of dates and end up fucking in a sleeping bag at Ocean Beach on New Year's Eve. It's 2000 now and a whole new century. If this hot Panamanian girl is any indicator, it will be a century of endless victory for yours truly.

Beach bonfire sleeping bag sex is problematic, however. Once you get a bunch of sand inside the bag, it only takes a few grains to get on the condom and riiiiipp! But I'm not to be trifled with. I've had beach sleeping bag sex before, being a horny, homeless teenager. Multiple times before, actually. So, to defeat these endless, hateful sand granules all around us, seemingly more numerous than the stars in the sky above us, I lay out a Tijuana blanket first, then roll the sleeping back in a measured fashion, so the mouth of it ends up over the center of the Tijuana blanket.

Then we take off our shoes at the edge, hop into the safety zone, and snuggle into a sort of cum-coon. I use the sinking of the sand to plant my knees, and I worm my way up into happiness and victory. "Ahhhhh!" I guarantee you this is the best homeless-style sex she's ever had. She has to bite my hawk tattooed chest to stop herself from alerting the other beach fuckers who is actually pulling this almost inevitable failure fiasco off.

Those poor, sandy-cocked suckers. That's why there are so many babies born in September, it's nine months after New Year's Eve. It's all those sandy, torn up, beach blanket bonfire condoms that popped on the fourth stroke of their cock and midnight. I'm in the clear, though, so bang-bang chicken wang! I squish and squirm into her pelvis with my meat worm until it finds the wetness.

The city possibly implodes into the dark ages from Y2K just on the other side of Golden Gate Park. We don't know, and we don't care. As long as there are some abandoned Walgreen's drug stores to smash into for Chunky Soup cans, beer, and condoms, then fuck it. We live here now. It's a new century, and I'm making a fresh start. So far, so good.

Itza is a pretty, young attorney, and now that we've been going out for a few months, I've moved into her house right by Dolores Park. Awesome! The downside is that she can't hide the fact that she's kind of uptight anymore. She's just now starting to get her bills from her NYU law school loans. She hates the corporate attorney job she has to have to pay for all that. Currently, she is defending the Beretta gun company, and it is killing her soul, but bills are bills. The story of most of our lives. Also, there's me, who didn't stop the worming and squirming on New Year's. At this point, I've wormed and squirmed all the way into her studio apartment. I wake up to her, staring at my face all the time. Not in that, "You're so beautiful when you sleep, type of way either."

When her parents come to town, I have to hide all of my belongings and vacate the premises. In the house, I'm paying half the rent in. She's good-hearted enough to prorate me for the week that I spend in the junky motel. When I ask about meeting her parents, she says, "Oh no, not with your drug convictions."

"For reals? For weed?" I query.

Her parents are immigrants that have never gone to sleep before putting in a ten-hour day, and they've instilled that work ethic in their only child. "Walk down the straight and narrow, and do not consort with trouble makers," I imagine they had her repeat as a child. She grew up in the all-white city of Clairmont, California, and spent most of her childhood in her room reading. That was one of the selling points. I like literate loners, and she is brilliant. I guess I'll try to stick it out.

Put a Pot on Every Burner

I start dabbling with the idea of being a stand-up comic during this time as a way of diversifying my storytelling options. A way to get my messages out to the people. Working in the Castro, I am struck by how the lesbians and the gays don't really hang out. After some observation, I come up with this little ode (full disclosure, it has been tweaked slightly at different times over the years, and the exact original version is, unfortunately, lost to time. This is pretty close to it, though. I came up with it after smoking a half joint of this beautiful weed called the *Bubba Kush*.) Here it is, my first stand-up bit:

People move to San Francisco and are surprised to find out that gay women and gay men have different bars, different restaurants, and they don't hang out together. Why? How could the diversity rainbow not unify these most likely friends in nature?

I'll tell you why! I was working the event where it all happened. It was a catering gig. I'm wearing a $45 tuxedo. I have to. Job requirement. I'm in charge of restocking the bar with fresh Zimas and nitrous canisters. The guy with the good coke is slicing smoked salmon and balancing it on crostinis with crème fresh and capers on the right side of the tranny burlesque dressing room…not the guy on the left side doing the same thing, his coke is bunk. The shit is good too! Gay coke. They don't fuck around in the Castro. We all have to be high. After all, it's The First Annual Gay Gala. An idea that's never been tried before.

Suddenly, the lesbians roll in, drunk off kombucha and American Spirit cigarettes, wearing wife beaters and Timberlands stained with deer blood. This happens just as my nostril starts dripping coke snot and parts of my frontal lobe all over my ratty, thrift store cummerbund. Clearly, I'm in no position to judge. Prince is just getting on stage. There are midgets in giant plastic hamster balls everywhere.

All the gay dudes turn away from an improvisational duet of "When Doves Cry" with a 2yo Katy Perry belting out her part from a jerry-rigged sex-swing turned bouncy chair. They are shocked at the audacity of these chicks' outfits, and they go for the lesbians! Even the lipstick ones! The first wave attacks! A dozen skinny Puerto Ricans with Versace *daisy dukes* and glitter traced nipples run-up to the lesbians and wave a "Power Bottoms Unite!" Banner in their faces yelling, "What the fuck is that?! Sears flannels and needle-nose plier belt holsters?! We're wearing bowties! It's a GALA!!! Barbara fucking Streisand just did a jumbo-screen Skype dedication to Harvey Milk on stage! How dare you come in here wearing less than dirt brown Oxfords and baggy acid wash jeans. Sean Penn Harvey Milk, you dumb sluts! WHY WOULD LIZ TAILOR WANT TO HANG OUT IN A HUNTING LODGE!?!?"

The lesbians bust out some strap-ons that even scare the power bottoms, who then run away shrieking. So now you know why there's one bar called The Rough Beaver and another bar called The White Swallow.

Planned Parenthood Power Trip

There is a time when Itza and I are in the closest thing she can be to love, and we're going to start having sex without a rubber. She wants me to go down to the clinic and get tested for the herps and the other assorted sex barnacles. I haven't had to do that in a while, so I ask her where she got her fluttery *love abalone* tested. She tells me Planned Parenthood, so that's where I go.

I have to pass through steel doors, then prove I'm not an anti-abortion terrorist through bulletproof glass. After showing ID and not seeming like an insane bible-nut, I'm admitted to the waiting room. Itza neglects to tell me that the only people that go to Planned Parenthood are girls that either got a fucked-up disease from a *man* or got knocked up and dumped by a *man*. I put this together from the stares of hatred being directed at me as I take a seat in the silent and somber waiting room.

After a few minutes I'm flipping through anti-male propaganda magazines such as *Women Up*, and *Oprah*. Soon, I get called into the back room by a short, stocky, mustachioed woman who looks pleased to meet me. Too pleased. I'm left alone in a room and told to put on a generic hospital gown and take a seat on the freezing stainless-steel stool. Everything else in there is also shiny metal, and the ultra-bright fluorescent light probes into every crevice to show that nothing has escaped sterilization. I wait for over ten minutes until Dr. Torture comes back, and she says, "Mr. Scales?"

"Yes," I timidly return, sensing some sort of inevitable doom.

"So, what type of services do you need today?"

"Well, my girlfriend and I would like to have sex without a condom, so I'd like a VD screening."

Then...I see something that terrifies me. I have no idea why I don't run away when Doctor Feel Bad pulls out this steel wire with a piece of cotton at the end. A wire she intends to ram down my pee-pee hole. Perhaps the horror has paralyzed me.

I am instructed to hold up my gown. I do it like a school girl wading into a cold lake for a baptism. She grabs on to my shrunken, frightened, confused willy and just shoves that fuckin' thing all the way down until it pierces my prostate gland. I can tell she is just *into it.* This is the *best* day of her life and the *worst* day of mine. I'm shrieking like a broken water hose in a Pontiac before she gets the thing in there. My memory is shaky after that. I'm gonna go ahead and say it's probably more of the same.

I leave, cold, ashamed, and semi-raped. I'm sitting, shivering at the bus stop, wondering if I should go jump off a bridge, unable to believe the invasion I've just endured. The excruciating pain. I tell Itza about the terror, and she seems sympathetic, but it appears like she's on the verge of giggling once or twice. The idea occurs to me that she may have set me up. She pets my shellshocked soldier and offers him a chance to tickle the pink salmon bead without a latex head laminator. Perhaps stick a finger in her filthy chocolatier. "I can't. He still hurts so bad," I tell her.

A week later, I see an ad on a bus stop that says you can go to the free clinic and get tested for almost every goddamn disease there is by pissing in a cup. Planned Parenthood fucked me! The agony rushes back, and I have to walk home.

Making the Movie

As the movie approaches, our relationship starts to sour, so I make Itza co-producer, thinking it will bring us together. We conduct auditions, interview potential crew members, I put the script together and all the other millions of preparations. Laduska and Mixt finished their tour and then recorded a bunch of stuff. So, I'm going to put *that* dope shit all over the soundtrack. After rereading the script I'd written in Mexico, I decide it does need work. Motormouth was right. *Shit.*

So, I just write a whole different one called Going Down. It's about a guy whose life is circling the drain, and he becomes convinced his dead girlfriend is making bad things happen to put him on the right path. By the end of the movie, he clenches his fists at the sky and says, "Alright, Penelope, you win! Next time you serve up morality soup, you think you could sprinkle a little less heart attack on mine!?"

I think I write this story to process seeing Kit's spirit out in the desert on that Mexican bus. The idea of our dead loved ones cheering us on is alluring. Perhaps there's no omnipotent god, but there could be that. There could be spirits *outside* our earthly bodies. We have proof they exist *inside* people's bodies, so at least we've *seen* them, you know? Who are *we* to assume they have to stay in us, right? Pretty self-centered and vain. Montecito Michelle worked *doggedly* to get her ass as hard as a diamond…you think she's going to just **let** her spirit walk away from that? Oh, hell naw.

Two days before we're supposed to shoot the motherfucking movie, I still have no place to shoot the elevator scene, so we decide to do it in our living room. That's the night we get in a big fight. She leaps on me from the top of the stairs, smashing my face into the ground. Damn near almost breaks my neck, and gives me carpet burn on my face. It's true love, people.

You can see that my face is heavily made up to cover the mess in the first half of the movie. Itza is not happy that I am going to just build an elevator in our living room. I don't see the big deal. "Why wouldn't you want a movie set and the cast and crew basically living with us for several weeks? It's a large studio apartment, Itza. Anything for your art, right? Oh, lawyers don't believe in that? Oh…well, why not?"

I eventually get her to settle down and go with it.

Now I just have to build an authentic looking elevator in my living room. No problem, I already have the purple carpet donated and waiting in the basement. Next, I go to the hardware store and pile all the plywood, plastic strips, and wood stain on a cart and bring it all up to the register. I pay the $150 for it and tell the cashier, "Listen, I gotta go find a ride to get this stuff back to the Mission District, watch it for five minutes, will you?"

The guy looks at me like I'm crazy, and I head out to the parking lot looking for a guy with a truck. What do you know? It's all trucks.

The first guy I see getting into one says, "No," to the offer of $20, and he looks at me like I'm crazy too. The second guy says, "No," as well. But the third guy says, "Yes."

I go back up to the register and grab the stuff in five minutes, just like I said I would. The perplexed cashier just looks at me and says, "Are you from New York?"

It's all arranged to start shooting tomorrow. We've done all the rehearsals, crew meetings, equipment is reserved the whole bit. I think everybody thinks I know what I'm doing, which is good. That's what I want. I want people to take this seriously. I can't sleep, so I go over the script again. I think I've slept ten hours in the last week. When the camera starts rolling, I'm the only one that ever has trouble remembering my lines—the writer of the script.

I'm a mess from doing the producing, set building, directing, script rewrites, and countless other things. Also, we couldn't fill the role of George Green, so I change the name to Georgia, and now Itza plays the part. Yay. Not. The grip finds out he's the only crew member not getting paid and starts dragging equipment across our hardwood floor.

On the second day of shooting the girl playing Julie falls through the elevator wall and starts crying, the camera guy records over a scene. By the third day, Itza and I are pretty much broken up.

—A few months from now, during a weeklong, dreary rain, in an editing room with a cranky old editor who is chain-smoking with the window barely cracked, whittling down all the tapes into usable clips, I can see the moment she breaks up with me in her mind. It was when I closed a glass door on her to stop having to listen to her talk. It was in between takes after the camera guy let it roll for an extra minute. Right there, the unmistakable look of a woman scorned. I say to Ed Jones, the Editor, "Delete the end of that one."

"Ok, bud." He says, cigarette *jiggle-dangling* in his pursed lips.

For now, I sleep in the living room on the purple carpeted elevator floor. At the end of every shoot day, I cook food or order out for the whole cast and crew. If it isn't for this, the crew, who I found on this innovative new website called Craigslist, would have walked out on me. They are being paid meagerly, if at all, and it's been a few weeks since I convinced them to work for half their usual rate on the basis that it's a good story. It's wearing off. Especially for the cameraman, who is working with his own digital video camera for just $100 a day.

The gaffer, i.e., lighting guy, Aron, is working for $60 a day even though he's just finished working on a David Arquette movie. This man retains a spectacular attitude throughout the shoot. The grip, as we know, is getting nothing. He is just sticking around to see me flounder. After our 10-hour days, I often cook, plate, and serve everyone's meals up personally. The grip first, to show that he matters to me even though I can't afford to pay him. I think this makes people willing to do their best when they see me doing things like that. I'm bubbling at the edges, though. Fried like an *over hard* egg.

I show up to work at the Republican gay bar and just bumble around dropping shit. My only regret about the overextension of my mind and body is it shows a little in my acting. Scenes that call for emotion are performed a bit flat. But overall, I gotta say, it's an entertaining movie; it only kind of sucks. Well worth watching, and that's what I'm aiming for. I'm a very self-critical artist, and if I had made a piece of shit, I would be the first to say it. So, the day after the cast and crew moves out of the house, and it's just Itza and me again, she breaks up with me…tells me I have 48-hours to move out of the house.

Two days after that, I get fired from my job because I heavily neglected it in preparation for, and in the shooting of Going Down. It appears I am living up to the title of my movie, like a real artist. So, there I am, all my belongings balanced on top of my skateboard, rolling down Valencia Street, past the spot I was run over by a cop car when I was 16, AWOL from a group home. It strikes me I shot the movie 40-yards from that very spot a decade later. I don't own that much stuff, and I never have. I am proud that when the shit hits the fan, I can stick it all on top of my skateboard and roll along jobless, homeless, at my most exhausted and broke point, girlfriendless, but still, somehow, happy as fuck.

It's true, I don't care. Because clutched tightly in my hand, at the top of my bundle, I have the tapes of Going Down. All those old tormentors who tore up my mom's teepee and whispered behind my back. All the angry, cold nights, I had to spend sleeping in somebody's car or a jail cell. The last little faded scraps of them that remain in me float out and up into the winds, to blow around aimlessly like I had done for so long. I've made my movie, and I know it's good! I know that **this** is what I was born to do, and I've done it. I made a movie! At this very moment, a block from 16th Street, it starts sprinkling on me and all my stuff. I know the digital videotapes are safe in their cartridges. I laugh like a maniac. A passing crack head mumbles, "Dese white boys cra-cra out heeeyah."

That's right, man. Crazy like a motherfucking henhouse fox. I roll on towards the corner in a squiggly but confident line as I push my skateboard saddled heap, determined, and undeterred.

About the Author

J.C. Scales—if you can believe this shit—is alive and well, living in a San Francisco rent-controlled apartment with his hot red-headed wife and his beautiful baby son. He has had to slow down a bit to survive. He just wants to live long enough to see Bezos actually start visiting the author's homes personally and flipping them upside down, vigorously shaking them for any change they may have been able to make authoring. Can't have the artist not suffering, can we? For some reason, we get our ideas only from pain and anguish. Doesn't that seem silly of us?

Coconut Fisticuffs is the second memoir by J.C. Scales. Please look for the first one, titled *The Goat Lady's Son and the Child Gladiators of Isla Vista*. If you'd like to tell him how you liked the book, go ahead and e-mail him at jcscales@yahoo.com. You wouldn't believe how much that would thrill him. He'd probably even respond. All right kids, go smash up a Bank of America!

Special thanks to Corinne Poulsen and Brandon Loberg. Oh! Oh! I almost forgot! The book's cover was drawn by Pot Plant Sarah's very talented 17yo daughter, Stella. Thanks, Stella!

Made in the USA
San Bernardino, CA
24 June 2020